EAST AND WEST INTERSECT
From the Orient to the Canadian Rockies

Say, "*Yes, Lord*," to the glory of God, and your
inner self will be renewed day by day.

Esther Fitzstevens

East and West Intersect: From the Orient to the Canadian Rockies

Trilogy Christian Publishers A Wholly Owned Subsidary of Trinity Broadcasting Network

2442 Michelle Drive Tustin, CA 92780

Copyright © 2022 by Esther Fitzstevens

Rights Department, 2442 Michelle Drive, Tustin, CA 92780.

Trilogy Christian Publishing/TBN and colophon are trademarks of Trinity Broadcasting Network.

Cover design by: Natalee Groves

For information about special discounts for bulk purchases, please contact Trilogy Christian Publishing.

Trilogy Disclaimer: The views and content expressed in this book are those of the author and may not necessarily reflect the views and doctrine of Trilogy Christian Publishing or the Trinity Broadcasting Network.

Not all photos sent to the author by family and friends were featured in the book. Esther Fitzstevens and her family apologize and appreciate everyone who has supported them.

Manufactured in the United States of America

10 9 8 7 6 5 4 3 2 1

Library of Congress Cataloging-in-Publication Data is available.

ISBN: 978-1-68556-667-8

E-ISBN: 978-1-68556-668-5

This book is a memoir. It reflects the author's present recollections of experiences over time. Some names and characteristics have been changed, some events have been compressed, and some dialogue has been recreated in many cases to protect the individuals, many of whom may face persecution. We hope this book inspires you.

TABLE OF CONTENTS

FOREWORD

Esther and John Fitzstevens have been dear friends. After John passed away in 2018, Esther set out to write the book you now hold in your hands: *East and West Intersect: From the Orient to the Canadian Rockies*. Their life experiences are worth reading—so much can be gleaned from this couple who served not only in war-torn countries but also in churches and ministries in the West.

John was distinguished, with quiet wisdom. Esther has an unforgettable personality and a vibrant smile that always lights up a room. She's one of the most caring individuals I've ever known. Throughout their lives, they showed love and compassion to all they encountered, no matter how difficult the circumstances. As you read, you will see the amazing work of a loving, compassionate Heavenly Father.

Our family's friendship with the Fitzstevens began before I was born. As a high school student, Esther met my parents when she attended an event to hear my father, Billy Graham, as a young preacher. She writes about this memory in the book. Then while in South Asia, the Fitzstevens met Bob Pierce, who was a mentor to me. He later encouraged me to look them up. I did, and a lifelong friendship began.

I was thankful when they moved to Boone, North Carolina, to work with me at Samaritan's Purse. Our staff loved and appreciated this special couple before they moved on to serve the Lord through other ministry opportunities. Years later, when they were considering "retiring" but told me they weren't ready to call it quits, I asked them if they would pray about moving to Croatia and overseeing a home we were establishing for young women. They said yes, and this home provided shelter and safety to young widows who had lost their husbands during the fighting in the Balkans and girls who had been raped by soldiers.

Through the Fitzstevens' story, I hope you will see how God can use ordinary lives in extraordinary ways. This book is relatable to those who, like John and Esther, give of themselves in service to others, whether it is overseas or at home with neighbors, friends, or family. It will inspire you to notice ways you can provide compassion or help to those who cross your path.

—Franklin Graham
President and CEO
Samaritan's Purse
Billy Graham Evangelistic Association

CHAPTER 1: MEETING THE GRAHAMS

I think it is only fitting to begin my story with how I met Ruth and Billy Graham, as I am nearing the end of my story, at ninety-three, working for their son, Franklin.

The first time I met Dr. Billy Graham was while I was in high school. Billy and Ruth would arrive on the bus in Clifton, New Jersey, from New York City, to speak at our youth rally. At that time, they were working closely with Brandt Reed, our HiBA (High School Born Againer's) Club leader, who held Tuesday night rallies throughout the metropolitan area high schools. We were all smitten by this dynamic newlywed couple and wanted to ride back to the bus station in Brandt's Model-T Ford with them.

Then there was the special rally at Madison Square Garden held once a year, and Billy Graham was the guest speaker for Jack Wrytzen (my mother spoke for him several times too). Since the high school team leaders were invited to sit on the platform, I had another chance to associate with Billy and Ruth.

Then many years later when Dr. Graham was invited, on numerous occasions, to speak to our troops in Vietnam at the big Air Force base. We would attend, and he would invite all the missionaries of the various mission groups to the military BOQ (Bachelor Officers' Quarters) for a meal. What a treat that was!

Franklin appeared on the scene through Dr. Bob Pierce, who had just handed over directorship of Samaritan's Purse to him. Dr. Bob was also the founder of World Vision and known for his compassion the world over for hurting people.

The first time we met Franklin, we were working in Hong Kong with the "boat people." He called and asked us to meet him since he was interested in our work with the Vietnamese refugees. Dr. Roberts, who worked under Dr. Bob and ran the office in California, had also told Franklin to call us. It was 10:00 p.m., and he was there on a layover with Jane, as they had just gotten married. It was a brief introduction in the lobby of the hotel.

Our second meeting with Franklin was when he came through town and observed our distribution of 500 cloth shoes. A Chinese friend had found them for less than a dollar a pair. The weather had turned cold, and the refugees were barefoot. Ha Jimmy, who was with Franklin, suggested the most efficient way to get this task accomplished would be to draw the outline of each shoe size on big sheets of cardboard. Then we had the refugees stand in line, placing their foot in the outline, at which time we handed them a pair from the respective stack.

Ha Jimmy had actually grown up next door to our MK (Missionary Kid) Dalat School in the Mission Tribal Center adjacent to our property. When Ha Jimmy heard the plight of the Vietnamese people, he connected up with Franklin as they both knew each other from North Carolina and felt constrained to go to Hong Kong with Franklin, and here we were, serving together...crisscross. His dad was one of the tribal church leaders who trained his fellow tribesmen to serve their own people in missionary service. Hundreds came to Jesus, and they, in turn, led hundreds of others to Jesus. Johnny, my husband, hired some of these Koho tribe people to work in the MK school. Their sweet, gentle spirit drew us all to them.

After we met the needs of these 500 refugees, Hong Kong Intelligence moved them off to an island camp where they were to be returned to China. These Chinese "refugees" had infiltrated the Vietnamese refugee migration as they came along the coast of China in search of fresh supplies. They had used this opportunity to get to another country along with the Vietnamese refugees, but on arrival in Hong Kong, their clothing, haircuts, money, and speech gave away their identity. When the time came for their departure back to China, they told the government they would not go until they were baptized! We had reached out to them ever since their Hong Kong days, getting permission to have local Chinese pastors go into the camps—Hong Kong and the island—to share Jesus. Their lives were transformed by the Good News of the Gospel. No one mentioned baptism to them, but in reading the Chinese Bibles we gave them, this was their desire!

The island camp officials called Johnny to come and baptize them. Johnny suggested immersing them at the beach. "Oh no, they'll escape via the ocean," they said. So, I gave Johnny a lovely brass bowl from Thailand our son David had given us for Christmas, and he sprinkled the 500. We were grateful to the Government Officials for granting their wishes. The Hong Kong officials began to open their hearts to the message of Jesus. What encouragement!

Our third visit with Franklin Graham was when Pastor Grout at First Alliance Church in Calgary, Alberta, where Johnny was an administrative pastor, invited Franklin to speak to a large men's group. Afterward, we invited him to our apartment, where I cooked him a Vietnamese meal. Preston Parrish, who often traveled with him, was there as well, so we enjoyed their fellowship over lunch.

One week later, Johnny left early to go to his office at the church to fast and pray, seeking God's leading in our future. At 6:30 a.m., the phone rang, and it was Franklin Graham asking Johnny to come to Boone and be the administrator! Three weeks later, two men from the church packed our truck and drove us south to Boone to begin our new ministry, with Johnny working as the administrator and me working in the World Medical Mission Department under Becky Williams' leadership. I loved doing the itineraries for doctors giving their time and talent to work overseas.

How blessed we've been these past thirty years of retirement to serve Him under such a dynamic, godly leader. He has grown Samaritan's Purse from only twenty employees in those early years to 1,259 domestic employees, 1,400 on the DART (Disaster Assistance Response Team) on-call roster, 296 International Field Staff, and over 2,500 National Staff (International Staff) with his vision for serving a hurting world. That's a lot of growth in thirty years!

While working in Boone, Franklin sent us back to Vietnam on a survey trip, which ended up with him moving us to Bangkok, where it would be easier to fly directly into Vietnam to do a monthly follow-up on many projects. We weren't allowed to live in Vietnam due to Communist control, but we had many friends there who had been in ministry with us from past years where we came alongside them to help and encourage them. Franklin has consistently worked alongside others in ministry, not concerned about accolades or recognition. This is what, we felt, set him apart from other organizations. This was just one of the reasons we felt so privileged to be a part of his work. In Bangkok, we had the added bonus of living near our son David and Karen, who are still ministering in Vietnam. It was an added blessing to be able to spend precious time with our grandsons, Ryan and Kyle. Ryan is now married to Naomi, who is a teacher in the same school where he is a counselor. They have two daughters, Laila and Miyoko. Kyle and Marley just had a baby boy. Marley is a nurse, and Kyle just got his doctorate in occupational therapy. I have four great-granddaughters and a great-grandson.

Franklin called at midnight one night to see how we were doing, never having any indication of our present situation. Johnny was in the hospital after having a heart attack on our return from Vietnam to Bangkok. Franklin immediately said I had to get Johnny home with specific instructions. When Johnny overheard our conversation, he told me to go to our apartment, and I would find an envelope in his jacket in the closet. (In the afternoon, he had taken it out of the guesthouse safe, as we were headed to Vietnam that week and would be paying for printing thousands of Vietnamese Bibles. He knew we'd be reimbursed.) So, I took the envelope, it was midnight, and the Bangkok alleys were dark. When I got to the airport, I hadn't even checked the envelope! When the ticket agent handed me the bill, I counted the money, and it was $10 more than the price of the tickets! I went back to the hospital, and the doctor gave me papers for Johnny to be released, and we were on the next flight to Nashville, where Franklin had contacted his famous surgeon friend. At midnight he was waiting for us, having delayed his vacation, and Johnny had his five-bypass heart surgery a few hours later.

While Johnny was in surgery, a plastic surgeon, who we had taken into Vietnam and wanted to return, called. After finding out about his open-heart surgery, he offered a place he had just purchased in North Carolina where Johnny could recuperate for a couple of months. Our first weeks after surgery, we were in a motel right near the hospital for Johnny to be near his doctor. I have a thing for Krispy Kreme doughnuts! Guess what was brought in fresh for the hotel guests every morning—Krispy Kreme doughnuts. I had my fix for those three weeks!

God orchestrated these events with precision to the point our family was even able to join us for a reunion while Johnny recuperated in Henderson, North Carolina. Franklin had even arranged for his pilot to get us from Nashville to Henderson. I know Donna, my daughter, shares in my gratitude to Franklin for not only saving Johnny's life but for always looking out for us and thinking of us when it came to opportunities to serve. I remember when she happened to be visiting us in Boone, and we were attending an SP and Billy Graham Association (BGA) function, she went up to him and expressed this. He was so gracious and warm. When she told me, "He even remembered me," I reminded her we had spent Thanksgiving with Jane, Franklin, and the boys when Jean Claude, her son, was just a month old. I had to smile when just recently, Jean Claude, who is now a psychiatrist in Alaska, expressed an interest in volunteering, down the road (if they could use him in any way), for Franklin's ministry, Heal Our Patriots, as he worked heavily with veterans suffering from PTSD in the VA Hospital as a resident. He has a real heart for vets. He told her, "He probably doesn't know me." To which I heard Donna reply, "You spent your first Thanksgiving at their home." Franklin and Jane and their now-grown sons have this unique ability to make people's lives they touch feel special, even though they are VIPs and super busy.

A month later, Franklin Graham had us on our way to Croatia. We had such peace knowing this was the place God had for us to serve. Our experience running the Saigon guesthouse for missionaries coming in from upcountry, sometimes facing medical needs, and running Dalat School for 150 missionaries' kids, not to mention in a war-torn country, had well equipped us for this next opportunity to serve.

Chapter 2: Nelly Bayer Meets Jacob Van Hine, Then Comes Marriage and Me in the Baby Carriage

> We live in the shadow of the Almighty sheltered by
> the God of all gods. This I declare, that He alone is
> my refuge, my place of safety, he is my God. For he
> rescues you from every trap and protects you from the
> fatal plague. He will shield you with His wings! They
> will shelter you. His faithful promises are your armor.
> Now you don't need to be afraid of the dark anymore
> nor fear the dangers of the day; nor dread the plagues
> of darkness, nor disasters in the morning.
>
> Psalm 91:1–6 (TLB)

I feel so blessed to have the heritage of being born to missionary parents who went to French Indochina, now Vietnam, in 1926. They met at the Missionary Training Institute in Nyack, New York. My mother, Nelly, was Swiss, and my dad, Jake, was second-generation Dutch.

So many ask me how my mother knew about Nyack. My grandfather, Emmanuel Bayer, a leading layman in the Brethren Church, was on a trolley car in Lausanne, Switzerland. He saw this lanky American couple that looked like missionaries, who were probably living in a boarding house and not being properly fed.

He found out they were studying French to go to Africa. So, he invited the Paul Freleighs to go home with him, where they could be properly cared for and continue their studies. As they learned French, my mother learned English and heard all about Nyack Missionary Training Institute.

At the end of that year, she graduated from high school, and her dad offered her a car or a trip to the United States as a graduation gift, and she chose the latter. Her brother, Bill, had gone to the States to open a family dry cleaning business in Asbury Park, New Jersey. She visited with him, went on to Nyack, and stayed on to study. She met my dad, and they were married three years later. John and Betty Stam, who they met during their internship at the Star of Hope Mission, were their best man and matron of honor. My parents went to Indochina under the C&MA, while John and Betty went on a different mission to China, where they were killed by bandits. Their baby daughter was rescued and hidden by her Chinese nanny, who finally got her to her family in the United States.

I was born in Hong Kong, as Mom's French doctor told her he would not deliver me during the outbreak of trichinosis in Hanoi, so they boarded a ship for Hong Kong. I was delivered during a typhoon! A few months after my birth, they returned to their mission station on the border of South China and North Indochina.

The house we lived in had the reputation of being haunted. Each night my dad locked the wooden shutters into the window frame. Without any catalyst, all the shutters would open simultaneously!

On one occasion, I was screaming in my crib. My parents described it as the cry of a wild animal, and nothing would console me. Finally, they prayed, and when they said, "In Jesus' name," I stopped! They found out the owner of our house was a Buddhist priestess conducting seances in the temple next door.

One day my dad was at his desk when a stone came from the corner of the ceiling across the room and landed in front of him. Strange! It was probably their first encounter with the power of darkness. My parents wisely moved shortly thereafter.

Since the government at the time was leery of foreigners, my parents introduced God to young people who came to their home through large, colorful scrolls depicting Bible stories. The young people would glue a picture to the large cardboard. Then they drew jigsaw pieces on the picture. The next step was to cut them out, mix them up, and then put them back together, as you would do a puzzle. It was a way of having a God-centered party with refreshments. That's how they shared Jesus, and many lives were forever changed.

Later my dad was able to minister to the opium addicts. I remember as a ten-year-old being fascinated as I would look down from my second-story bedroom window into the opium den next door. Little did I know my life would crisscross with one of the men's granddaughters years later in a Dutch Reformed Church in Oak Park, Illinois. This church had been giving towards our support when we were working with Samaritan's Purse and going into Vietnam. Franklin would send us to speak during their annual missions conference. One time I was in the lobby and introduced myself to a Vietnamese lady. I asked her how she became a Christian, and my heart skipped a beat when she told me her grandfather, who was an opium addict, found the Lord through Jake Van Hine. One by one, each member of the family came to Christ. She was so excited to find out he was my dad. I couldn't believe it when I met her husband, who is the nephew of dear missionary friends of ours from Laos, the Sawyers.

My parents Jake and Nelly Van Hine
to French Indochina 1926

Chapter 3: In His Safekeeping

In His safekeeping:
- A. Opium ring and lemonade poisoning
- B. Japanese invasion
- C. Escape to Hong Kong with a Japanese bomber flying overhead

"The Lord is on my side; I will not fear. What can man do to me?" (Psalm 118:6, ESV)

Sometimes my dad and I would reminisce about our early days in Vietnam and of God's protection. One incident was when my dad had traveled up close to the China border to bring God's Word to those villages. At night, he'd sleep in a local village hut. One morning, sitting on the edge of the wooden bed, he felt a package taped to the slats on the underside of the bed. He saw it was a cache of opium. On the return home to Lang Son, he reported it to the officials and found out he had unearthed a drug ring.

Weeks later, when my mother was in Hanoi at Dr. Patterson's clinic, my dad and I were walking home, and a man came toward us. He blurted out in amazement, "What! Are you still alive? I put enough poison in your lemonade to kill an elephant." When we checked with our cook, he said a stranger had come in to visit him in the kitchen, a separate unit behind our house, and the lemonade was there, ready to be served for supper. When my dad took a sip of the lemonade, he thought it tasted strange and told me immediately to put the glass down and not to touch it.

Ten years later, the Japanese came across the Chinese border into our town of Lang Son. I was returning from Dalat, where I attended mission school nine months out of the year. So, my parents left to meet me in Hanoi. Prior to their departure, they packed all our belongings to go on furlough. After leaving my mother and me in Hanoi, Dad returned to retrieve everything. He was met by the Japanese soldiers on the outskirts of town and held at gunpoint. They instructed him to stay, and they would come back with our trunks. It was nightfall when they returned, wanting him to sign papers that he had received all his possessions. He told them he would not sign anything until he saw the contents of the trunks, our treasures. One treasure was my Grandmother Bayer's solid silver European place settings that had approximately ten different pieces for fifteen settings. They replied, "Sign, or else…" with a bayonet poking into his ribs, "there's nothing we love more than killing people!"

It wasn't until my dad joined us in Hanoi at our mission station he found the trunks packed solid with garbage, empty milk cans, and wood from the backyard. On the very top of one of the trunks was an old picture of my dad where they had taken a bayonet and slashed it through his heart, and under that was my Grandfather's Swiss Bible.

We got the last ship out to Hong Kong on a loaded oil tanker. Our cabin was in the crew quarters on the back of the ship, which the captain reluctantly let us have and moved his crew elsewhere. The deck was level with the ocean. Waves crashed the deck with typhoon force, so we had to be taken by the arm to get to the dining room without being swept out to sea. Since my dad didn't have the strength, Mr. Lang, a Chinese missionary, took his place.

Daily, a Japanese bomber swooped over the ship. It was close enough that I could see the bombs lying in their racks. I recognized the same pilot each day and would wave to him as I hung my head over the railing, not realizing the danger we were in. One bomb would have blown us out of the water! When we arrived in the Hong Kong harbor, our sober sea captain, who had stayed drunk the whole trip, expressed how grateful he was we were on board ship, acknowledging it was our God who sailed us through the Japanese blockade and typhoon weather to Hong Kong.

Chapter 4: Meeting Johnny, the Love of My Life

"Satisfy us in the morning with your steadfast love, that we may rejoice and be glad all our days" (Psalm 90:14, ESV).

My parents were not able to return to Indochina as the war between the French and the Vietminh was at its peak. They made a home for me in Clifton, New Jersey, and my dad worked in the C&MA headquarters in New York City in the finance department. This was his field of work before he answered God's call to the mission field.

I loved my high school years and was very involved in my school and church. I was always grateful for my Christian heritage, but there came a time when I was very aware I needed a personal relationship with Him through Jesus, who loved me so much that He died on the cross for my sins and gave me the gift of salvation. This is the message of faith in Jesus that I was committed to sharing throughout my life. When people asked me about the joy and love I demonstrated toward others in my work, I was cognizant of the fact it was impossible for me to do any of it in my own strength or with my own resources. So, it made it so much easier to give God credit and hopefully make them think of Him as our provider in all things.

Just before I graduated from high school, my parents took me to Nyack for commencement weekend. This was where I would be a student in the fall. The president of the senior class invited three of us girls out after class night along with two of his friends. I didn't know that he, Bob, had asked Johnny to drive his car so he could be with me. The other two girls had their eyes on Bob and Jerry, so that left Johnny! After they pointed him out to me earlier that day, I thought, *Wow! I'll be glad to be his date.* He had just been discharged from the army in France and Germany. We got to the car and were standing around awkwardly, so I moved to the backdoor, figuring Johnny would be sitting in the backseat. He moved toward me and put his arm up against the door divider when Bob pushed up against it. So, Johnny was able to jump in! That blind date was the miracle of my meeting Johnny, originally from Miami. We connected both mentally and spiritually. He came to my high school graduation in New Jersey a few days later. My mother commented, "You're in love, aren't you?" And I was! She had been in the orient too long, where arranged marriages were an accepted practice, and she had arranged a marriage for me. So, she was not excited to hear I was in love with another guy.

Johnny went to Nyack for summer school, making up time after coming out of the army and losing the first semester at the college. After I finished my first semester, we were engaged. When he asked me if I would go with him to the mission field, I gladly said yes. I didn't realize that meant China, as he had been drawn to Chinese pilots stationed in Mississippi when he was in the Air Force.

When I went forward at missionary service in college and told the Lord I would go anywhere, even if it meant China, I did not realize how soon I would be tested. One doesn't make glib promises to God. I really feared the Chinese people because of an early experience as a child in Indochina when I was close to being kidnapped by a group of men involved in white slavery, who were taking girls across the border from our town into China, just a few miles away. I knew I had to get over my fear of the Chinese. So, each Sunday for my practical work assignment, I went to Chinatown, New York, to teach little children Bible stories while their parents studied English. I wondered how I ever could have feared the Chinese… it was a wonderful experience.

When our mission leaders interviewed Johnny and me for overseas ministry, we were assigned to China, but a few years later, the doors to China closed, and they asked us if we would be willing to go to Indochina! Awesome! I realized I had to be willing, and then God gave me the desires of my heart.

Chapter 5: Friends and Family

"Every morning tell him, 'Thank you for your kindness,' and every evening rejoice in all his faithfulness. [...] You have done so much for me, O Lord. No wonder I am glad! I sing for joy. O, Lord, what miracles you do! And how deep are your thoughts!" (Psalm 92:2–5, TLB)

Johnny's sister Ruth and her husband, Don Olson, live down the road from me in John Knox Village. They have been so faithful in demonstrating their love over the years as we traveled back and forth from Vietnam and throughout the years. Their home was always open to us in Maryland. Don, who was head of the dental department at Johns Hopkins University, even made sure the kids' dental needs were met. One time he lined the kids up in chairs and had his students work on them under his supervision. This was much needed with dental care being very limited in Vietnam. When we were in Nyack on furlough prior to this, and he had a practice in New City, he made sure we were well taken care of.

Don and Ruth also took in several Vietnamese refugees. They lived with them for quite some time while they helped them find work, housing, and furnishings. They were so giving not only of their time but extra love and attention. Ruth is the same today.

Before COVID-19, she was always visiting lonely people in our village, as she grew up in Miami and had many friends where I lived. I know she does the same in her community.

We became good friends with the Ericksons in Vietnam and stayed in touch when they returned to the States. Their home was always open to us as well. Bev and Donna were good friends in first grade. Bev saw how the girls in their room bullied Donna when she would visit us in the boy's dorm on weekends and defended her. This was something Donna was so grateful for. Unfortunately, the bullying followed Donna, so we were really happy when we lived in Saigon to find a school run by Shell Oil Company, so she didn't have to go back to Dalat when it moved to Malaysia. By that time, we were working with Christian Children's Fund (CCF), so we had flexibility in where the kids could attend school. Another intersection in my story was Ruth Erickson's dad, Mr. Mills, the founder of CCF. Gale Erickson told Mr. Mills about Johnny, and we ended up working for them. The government in Vietnam was so pleased with the fact children were getting the help they needed they gave Johnny an award, as well as an award for Johnny's support of war widows. The government officials loved award pinning ceremonies! Johnny also built schools and clinics in these communities and had feeding programs for the children. Feeding the hungry was Johnny's passion.

I was involved in translating letters for the Stateside sponsors of the children. A special occasion was when a GI stationed in our area wanted to meet the child he had been supporting. He came with gifts, and I served as his interpreter. It was a very moving experience.

We loved helping the GIs any way we could. They knew they were always welcome in our home, especially at mealtime. One time I remember Steve Guckenheimer almost turning green as he ate some chocolate cookies I had just baked and disappeared in a hurry. Since he was at the house often, I asked him what happened, and he said when the breeze came in from the fish market down the street, he could taste the fish as if it was in the cookies. Steve used to teach English at the Youth Center a couple of nights a week with me, and we are still friends along with his wife, Marsha.

I met the Branaghs the summer after meeting Johnny. It had already been planned that I would go to California while my parents packed to leave for Indochina. I enjoyed my summer working as a waitress at Mount Hermon Conference Center near Santa Cruz. My last week there, the staff put on a program for the guests, and I was asked to give my testimony since that night, my parents were leaving for the mission field.

A sweet lady told me she had met my mother some years before when my mother spoke at her church. She gave me her phone number and told me to call her if I was ever in the area and needed a place to stay. It was my last day at Mount Hermon, and I still did not have a ride to San Francisco, where I was to get my flight to New York and on to Nyack. A friend came to my rescue, but I still did not have any lodging. Then I remembered Mrs. Branagh's offer—a miracle transpired! She told me how her telephone had not been working for days. She happened to go by and heard a slight click and decided to pick it up, and it was me! I had a few wonderful days with her family. She took me shopping, and I had a lovely wardrobe to start college. Her husband, a big contractor, offered to pay my way through Nyack—another miracle! They were like my family throughout the years that followed as we were in and out of their home. Their son and daughter-in-law, Charlie and Nat, took over when Uncle Charlie and Aunt Lottie passed.

I was doubly blessed to have such a dear friend in Nat, who was such an inspiration to me. She still drove me to go shopping, even in her nineties. Her mind was sharp until the day the Lord took her home.

The Lord blessed us with other close friends, Col. Dee and Jackie Pettigrew, who the US Army assigned to Dalat, where Dee was the US attaché to the West Point of Vietnam. Their son, Chip, and daughter, Jenny, attended our school for missionary kids (MKs). Chip went on to West Point and became a surgeon. He went to South America often, donating countless hours performing surgery on those who so desperately needed him.

Johnny and I were so happy when Dee offered to become advisor to our high school Boy Scouts. They loved having a man of his stature as their leader. Jackie was always helping out. One time she had all the girls over to her house to see a reel-to-reel movie on Jackie Kennedy giving a tour of the White House. She entertained with such class! Their home was always open to us missionaries, and we loved our times there.

We selfishly treasured our time as a family with them during our school break, sitting around their fireplace, playing board games. I find it remarkable Jackie has never missed a month in supporting our work for over sixty years.

One time I was scheduled to speak at a women's luncheon for Greg Laurie's Calvary Chapel in Riverside, California. My plane had been diverted to another city, but my hostess, Debbie Darling, drove the two hours to get me. She took me to their home and watched me unpack. The next thing I knew, she was taking me shoe shopping. I immediately went to the cheaper quality shoes, and she dragged me over to the expensive shoes and proceeded to pick out a $150 pair. I objected profusely, saying they were too expensive. She looked at me and said, "Esther, I want to buy you these shoes, so just let me!" She then challenged me and said something to the effect of, "Even if you don't think you deserve them, I do!" She taught me a valuable lesson on self-worth.

I am reminded of Psalm 139 and how it was hard for me to read it out loud and really mean it because I came from the generation where if I said I was "wonderfully made," it might be considered pride. After reading it out loud several times, though, I felt as though something changed in me. Really, it was Debbie that triggered the change initially. Years later, I was back, speaking in the same area, and when someone asked me how I knew Debbie, I lifted my shoes up from under the table! I wore them for years, and they never did wear out.

Mary Sofield is another dear friend I met in Saigon when her husband was stationed with the US embassy. She came to visit us at our MK school and treated all sixty girls to lovely haircuts. Later, when Norm passed, she married Sam Vause, who also became a dear friend. They were always so willing to open their home to us when we were in the USA. Deb, Mary's daughter, has always been so supportive and good to us, even opening her home in Greenville when we needed a place for several months while in transition.

Mary and Sam even hosted our son Mel and Linda's wedding in their beautiful home. One time when we were in Europe, we went to our good friend's home for dinner, Micheline and Maitre Lambert. In conversation, Mary realized her apartment was above Maitre Lambert's law firm office in Saigon, and he had handled David, Mary's son's adoption. What a small world!

One time while overseas, we left our car in Sam and Mary's parking lot, and a big branch fell and caused a dent in our fender—this was an act of God. Fast forward to Florida. For months when we drove the dented car, I always felt embarrassed, especially when driving up to speak at a church! Johnny would always say, "Who cares? It's just your pride!"

One day, missionary colleagues, Grady and Evelyn Mangham, offered to take us to a good Vietnamese car repair shop that belonged to the Tes. As we pulled in, they came out and asked me if I knew a Mrs. Vinh as they had been looking for her for years! I told them I was Mrs. Vinh! In refugee camps, it was an abbreviation of Fitzstevens, a name too hard to pronounce. So Vinh was short for "ven." Mr. and Mrs. Te started crying because they had been asking all their friends about an American lady with the name of Vinh and were told, "There is no such person."

I remembered Mr. Te from Hong Kong, who had lost track of his son in the refugee camp because he had been air evacuated off the little boat they were on, as his son, Tri, was very ill. Mr. Te asked me for help in finding Tri. So, I found out through the prison department where sick children were taken. I was then able to find this little, scared boy. At first, he was stunned, trying to figure out who this white lady was speaking his language. Then I was able to tell him his mom and dad were waiting for him, so he needed to eat and get strong. Shortly thereafter, he was reunited with his family. This was the beginning of many other tearful reunions that God allowed me to facilitate. Mr. Te was such a blessing to me in the refugee camps and became my right arm, assisting in many projects like the distribution of clothing and running the video *Life of Christ Series* in different parts of the camp he was in.

We became close friends and often stopped in to visit at their repair shop in Winter Haven, which was just a half-hour from where we lived in Kissimmee, Florida. This "little boy" became a good friend of our family. We then met his wife, Lan, who he had brought back from Vietnam. We are now watching their baby grow into an adorable six-year-old.

Don and Vicki Howe have been good friends as well. Vicki wanted all of her ten children to be exposed to missions and visited every time they came to Kissimmee to visit Don's mother. They are such prayer warriors. One time they came over for a dinner of leftovers as we were hunkered down in guest housing in one of the Good Samaritan's block apartments in case the storm hit. Jean Claude, Donna's son, called concerned about not having an appointment for an interview for residency. We all prayed together, and he got a call the next morning saying they had a cancellation and would he be interested in an interview.

Ruth and Don Olson

Steve Guckenheimer,
a frequent visitor

Col. Dee Pettigrew volunteer to
our Dalat School Jet Cadets

Chapter 6: Marriage, Two Years of Alabama Home Service, Then Switzerland

"Let us see your miracles again; let our children see glorious things, the kind you used to do, and let the Lord our God favor us and give us success" (Psalm 90:16–17, TLB).

Three big events took place at the beginning of June 1950. Johnny graduated from Geneva College, Beaver Falls, Pennsylvania. I graduated from Nyack, and we were married that same evening. Dr. Shuman, President of C&MA, who had married my parents, took part, and Dr. Gilbert Johnson, a professor at Nyack, married us. He and his wife had been like parents to me through the years growing up when my parents had other assignments and were unable to take care of me. They had been roommates with my parents while in training at Nyack and had no children of their own. I was so grateful to the Lord for having them in my life until they passed away at Shell Point Village years later.

With graduations and the wedding being over, we were assigned to our first pastorate in Jasper, Alabama. It was an impoverished area of Alabama. One of the few ladies in the church that had a job invited us for Sunday dinners for real southern cooking. Her fried chicken was on a par with my mother-in-law's, also from the

Deep South. Our congregation was composed of a few adults and mostly children. One day a little girl, one of twelve children, was at our door with just a rag tied around her waist. It was winter too. "Preacher, my mommy has no money to feed us and wants me to ask you to help." I knew Johnny had our last five dollars in his shirt pocket, and of course, he gave it to her. Our payday was a week away ($40 a month!), and we knew we had a faithful God who was always there for us and right on time. After all, we were candidates for the mission field, and this was our two-year training program.

We had numerous tests. When our son David was born, there was a time when there was no milk for his bottle. One afternoon, Johnny stopped at the post office, hoping he'd find a dollar or two in the mail since friends knew our situation. There wasn't anything. When we stopped again on the way to the prayer meeting, there it was. The postman told us he had put the envelope in the wrong box and found it just before we got there. God is always on time! Before getting to church that evening, we stopped at the little corner store, bought a can of evaporated milk, and poured it into David's bottle that I had half-filled with water in faith! The owner of the store said we could have charged the milk earlier in the day, but we said we couldn't do that, and God honored our faith.

There were times when we had empty shelves, having used even the last bit of flour and oil for biscuits. Those lessons of God's faithfulness carried us through many years of ministry.

What a contrast the next two years were when we lived in Geneva, Switzerland, attending the university in preparation for our career in French Indochina. We loved the beauty of the country and enjoyed getting to know my mother's family, uncles, aunts, and cousins, where we could practice our French.

As we traveled on to France one and a half years later and we embarked on the ship in Marseille that would get us to our final destination, we thought we would have further opportunity to practice our French. We didn't see the usual twelve passengers that freighters carry. Instead, there were 400 sheep being transported to Indochina to feed the Muslim Moroccan troops fighting for the French army! The real passengers were the Moroccan soldiers, the sheep's shepherds.

Going through the Suez Canal was desert, and it was very still, no breeze. The flies accumulated by the thousands so that when we ate, we needed one hand free to fan the flies from our forks!

In Saigon, we picked up another passenger: an elephant for the zoo in Haiphong! One day he got loose and ran through the halls only to get his back cut up by the ceiling light bulbs! All these animals on board the ship fascinated our three-year-old David.

Our big day 1950

My Swiss family when I was a little girl

CHAPTER 7: FRENCH INDOCHINA—LEARNING VIETNAMESE

"But the loving-kindness of the Lord is from everlasting to everlasting to those who reverence him; his salvation is to children's children of those who are faithful to his covenant and remember to obey him" (Psalm 103:17, TLB).

What a thrill it was for me to be back in French Indochina and for Johnny to get acquainted with the new culture and the people that I loved. Our first assignment was two more years of language study, this time—Vietnamese. For me, it was easier as my childhood knowledge of the language came back to me, but we still both studied eight hours a day with the tutor. After six months, my tutor asked me if I was ready to give a lesson at the children's meeting at the church. I studied and memorized for days.

The day finally came, and it went well until I threw in a closing sentence that was not planned. I thought I said, "I hope you have understood." They all started snickering and giggling, and some were doubled over with laughter! Let me insert here that every word has six tones, each with a different meaning, and some sound very much alike. "I hope" was *ước ao*, an even tone, and I said an up tone *ướt áo*, meaning "I wet my dress." As my tutor and I walked home, I asked her what I had said. She asked me if I really wanted to know! I never wanted to make that mistake again! We had a good laugh. When Vietnamese say their language is easy because it is made up of one-syllable words, it's the tones that are the killer. Here are two illustrations: the word for mother is *mẹ*, a guttural tone, and the word for ghost is *ma an* even tone. So, you could be calling for a ghost when you thought you were calling your mom. The word *Chúa*, a high tone is "God," even tone *chua* means "sour," and a down tone *chùa* is "temple," usually a Buddhist temple. So, you can see the problems that easy mistakes can cause. One day, I asked our house helper when he came back upstairs to bring me the ink (*mực*, low tone), but he brought me the jam (*mứt*, high tone). He just took me literally, not thinking I was at my desk, and why would I want jam?

I feel blessed to speak French and English, along with the Vietnamese I picked up as a child playing with kids on the street and the local preacher's kids (my best friends). So, I learned three languages simultaneously. My heart is always warmed when I get a call from one of my oldest best friends, who is now a pastor's wife in California. Her sister married a pastor who lived around the corner from us when we lived in Saigon. I hadn't seen them for years. Then one time, I was sitting in the same pew I sat in as a child in the Hanoi church, where we visited from our mission station in Lang Son. I looked at the couple sitting next to me, and I had to do a double-take. It was them! She leaned over and said, "You're Esther." They were also visiting from the US. We had to be careful as we were under the scrutiny of the Communists. So, we couldn't hug each other and had to hide our exuberance over this "chance" encounter. It was bittersweet. An elderly gentleman also braved a "hello" and whispered he knew my parents, "*Ong Bà Van Hine.*" I was so moved.

The reason I also consider French as a mother tongue is because the French part of Switzerland was my mother's homeland! In my early years, the French governed Vietnam, so their children were also my playmates. In later years, I had the privilege of using these language skills to teach Vietnamese and French to the children of the American army, civilian, and embassy advisors, along with the children of missionaries. When I taught French at the Shell Oil Company school in Saigon, the leadership asked me to teach Vietnamese culture alongside the language in an effort to prevent fights. A typical fight might ensue; for example, if an American child got hurt, the Vietnamese cultural response would be laughter so as to not attract attention from the evil spirits. The irony of this situation was the Vietnamese kids were actually laughing in order to distract the evil spirits from further harming them. Once the American kids understood this, it made a big difference. It also contributed to the bigger picture of changing the local persona of the American oilfield personnel.

Chapter 8: Montreal and the Mayor

"Now then, take your weapons, your quiver and your bow, and go out to the field and hunt game for me" (Genesis 27:3, ESV).

During our years in Vietnam, we had the privilege of serving in Phan Thiết. A Vietnamese colonel and his family invited us for a picnic, and later in the day, he took us to a pond where there were a lot of animal tracks. He had a mirador built up in a tree, a platform where at dusk, we could sit and wait for the animals to come for a drink. I found it hard to squat up there, and finally, I dropped my legs over the edge. Johnny spotted my white socks and exclaimed, "You're going to spook all the animals!" My hunting career was short-lived. The colonel came by to check and saw he needed to take me to a local village house where I was given a hard, wooden bed, highly polished for special family gatherings and special guests. I can assure you I didn't sleep a wink that night.

I heard gunshots in the distance and that morning saw they had been able to kill a leopard that had been stalking the villages, and there was also a 700 lb. deer on the back of the jeep that we took home and dressed so we could share it with everyone. We ended up happy with a two lb. piece of venison. Johnny also hunted in Dalat to help the tribespeople with food. One time the local police threw him in jail. When he asked to come home to take a shower, he called our friend, the mayor, who was upset with the police and told them to release him.

Years later, when we were living in Montreal, where the government had taken in hundreds of refugees, I got a knock at the door, and guess who it was? The mayor! He didn't even engage in the usual formalities but blurted out, "I want to know Jesus!" He said as a child, he had lived in Cambodia and heard Mrs. Hammond, one of our missionaries, teach the children about Jesus, and he sang for us "Jesus Loves Me" that she had taught him. His heart was longing for the peace Jesus gives.

The mayor had purchased a Vietnamese grocery store in downtown Montreal, and we often dropped into the grocery shop to encourage him.

CHAPTER 9: VC AMBUSH IN BÉN TRE

"Hide your loved ones in the shelter of your presence, […] safe from all conspiring men. Blessed is the Lord, for he has shown me that his never-failing love protects me like the wall of a fort" (Psalm 31:20–21, TLB).

After Phan Thiết, we moved South to Bến Tre, which was the hotbed of Vietcong control. Johnny continued to be led into areas that were dangerous as he came alongside our Vietnamese pastors to evangelize the surrounding villages. One night, Johnny felt constrained not to go out. I was shocked that he said no to the pastors. I thought, *He's lost his zeal for God.* I was disappointed because I loved teaching the children stories from the Bible.

Early the next morning, our pastor was at our door saying that the VC[1] were behind every coconut tree, out to get us. They called out as the pastors were headed back in the dark. "Where are the American people?" "God spared your lives," the pastor said. "God led you not to go with us last night." Again, "But God!"

On a trip to a village, Johnny and the pastors asked the Buddhist monk if they could set up their projector to show the *Life of Christ* on the white wall of their temple. The monk was so moved

---

1. This term refers to Vietcong, the guerrilla force army of South Vietnam.

that night that he and his wife accepted Jesus! A day or so later, she was bitten by a poisonous snake, and the men prayed, and she was healed—a live demonstration of God's power.

The owner of our house was a doctor, who married into a French family, and when he built his house, he was not allowed to live in it because it was larger than the local governor's mansion. Thus, we were only charged $30 a month in rent.

The Garth Hunts lived with us their first few months of initiation on the field. Garth didn't like finding bats under his bed, hanging from the wooden slats where it was dark in the daytime. When evening came, he would walk up our winding staircase holding a magazine in front of his face and over his head to protect himself from the bats flying through. Johnny used a tennis racket in the small bathroom to get them off their radar, and they'd go crazy. At first, this made Garth really nervous, but then he got to the place where he could laugh with us about it, and we'd laugh about how it just became everyday life to us.

I had an experience in the church watching a bat flying around, and it landed on the pastor's neck. When I saw that, I found it hard to believe what Johnny had told me that they wouldn't bother me, as I used to duck when they'd swoop down over our dining room table. The table was halfway through their route from our big open front door to the back.

One day, a large group of women was yelling at us outside our house, accusing us of kidnapping their missing children and keeping them in our nonexistent basement. We lived on the Mekong River, where the huts were built on stilts over the river. Young children fell in the river, went missing, and we were accused.

Our big house was used for youth rallies as young people came in from all over the area. I remember making raised donuts by the hundreds, and they loved it.

On Sundays, we would visit one of the thirteen Vietnamese churches in our area of ministry. One Sunday, we were in the church surrounded by canals. Johnny was preaching, and I was at the organ and suddenly noticed five-year-old David was missing! I slipped out the door close by and found him. He had gotten a string and a bamboo stick and was on a little bridge that was really the toilet and was feeling like he was fishing.

At one point, David needed a tonsillectomy, and we were so grateful he wouldn't be having it in a local hospital as they wouldn't give anesthesia. One of our colleagues, Ed Thompson, had a hair-raising story of his son's experience. We were so grateful that our mission doctor, Dr. Vietti, agreed to do the surgery at the leprosarium in the jungle area near Banmethuot, where we were visiting friends. What should have been a simple procedure took more than two hours. First, the big ceiling surgery lamp didn't work, and Clyde Powell had to go search for a hunting light that the doc could attach to her head. Then something went wrong with the anesthesia, and David ended up with an overdose. As they were cleaning up, they found a live cobra curled up under the operating table right where Dr. Vietti had been standing. Think what could have happened to the doctor if she had been bitten by the cobra and jerked the instrument while doing the procedure, and what could have happened to David!

Dr. Vietti was later captured by the Vietcong and was never seen again during these many years, along with Archie Mitchell and Dan Gerber.

When it was all over, Johnny picked David up and took him to a bed in the next room to rest. Before returning to Powell's home, Johnny picked David up to find him sleeping next to the second cobra, as cobras go in pairs, and they are poisonous! But God spared him again! But there were people praying. Johnny was in Ohio, and a couple at a church asked if he remembered what happened in Vietnam on a certain night, at a certain time. He told them the above story, and they said they were awakened in the night to pray for an extended time, a couple of hours, and that was it! So, when God wakes you up, pray!

Another prayer warrior was Johnny's mom. When Johnny was a baby, God spared his life when he had a serious problem with his adenoids. The doctor hadn't given him much hope. Johnny's mom went to the neighbor next door, where they prayed for God's healing, and a few hours later, when the doctor returned to find Johnny playing in the playpen, he recognized God had performed a miracle.

Johnny had another miracle when he was just five months old. The Great Hurricane of Miami hit his home, and it became necessary for his parents to evacuate across the street to a brick building. Along the way, Johnny's mom couldn't hold him due to the strong winds, and when they made it inside the door of the brick building, John Sr. noticed he wasn't in her arms. He dashed back out to find him in the street. This was indeed miraculous that he was even able to maneuver through the monumental winds, much less find Johnny.

Recently I had just been discharged from the hospital, and although I was weak, my instincts told me to make my usual calls to Samaritan's Purse Donors. When I came to a donor named "Minh Lê," I thought, *This is a Vietnamese name.* So, I left a voicemail starting out in English and ending in Vietnamese. When she returned my call, her husband entered the room and asked who was on the phone. She scribbled my name on a piece of paper, and it immediately jogged his memory. His dad often mentioned our name, telling him these missionaries sacrificed for our people. Sixty years ago, "America" represented paradise for us. Who would leave the comfort of their home, come to this poor country, learn an obscure language, and learn a strange culture in order to bring the Gospel to a people they didn't even know? "This is agape love in action," she said. I was moved by this, but it was only as an affirmation that God had laid it on our hearts to do this because I had never looked at it from this perspective.

It was the common denominator, Ben Tre, where we served, and Thomas' grandfather pastored that initiated a crisscross from west to east, America to (Ben Tre) Vietnam, then California to Florida. Only God could orchestrate our meeting with the wave of His baton. In His orchestra, He brings us together, His instruments, to create perfect harmony, giving Him honor, glory, and praise.

I asked Minh Lê and Thomas where they were attending church, and they said, "Chuck Smith's Calvary Chapel." I couldn't believe it! I shared how I had been a good speaker for his wife, Kay. Then when we were working in Croatia, they'd invite us up to Austria to their retreat center. We were blessed to experience their R&R center, a breather from our hectic schedule, and were privileged to sit under Chuck's Bible teaching—a real time of physical and spiritual renewal.

God not only gave us one but two common denominators, Ben Tre and Chuck Smith, that prepared us for the day we would meet and be immediately cognizant of His orchestration that made East meet West, crisscrossing our lives.

Chapter 10: Johnny Gets Master's in Education from Stetson

"And my God will supply every need of yours according to his riches in glory in Christ Jesus" (Philippians 4:19, ESV).

At one point, we felt we needed to stay home an additional year after being in the states for furlough for the kids' stability and for Johnny to get his master's degree. The first thing Johnny did was to call the Alliance asking for a leave of absence, which meant our monthly allowance would be cut as of that day. That's when our walk of faith was strengthened. Everything fell into place when he applied for a $1,000 scholarship that helps missionaries and received it that very day. Jo Beck, a pastor friend from the Deland C&MA church, said he thought Johnny could get accepted at Stetson University and knew of a three-bedroom house that would be vacant for a year with rent of only $30 a month. Without my parents knowing any of these details, they called that night saying they were stepping out in faith to give us $30 a month for our rent, not knowing we had found a house to rent for $30 that day. I sold Avon and spoke in churches and clubs as Vietnam was in the news a lot, and God supplied all our needs. A year later, we were all headed back to Vietnam with Johnny's thesis on Dalat School in hand.

Chapter 11: Tet Offensive

"The angel of the Lord encamps around those who fear him, and delivers them" (Psalm 34:7, ESV).

Several years later, before the Tet Offensive took place, we were living in Saigon. There was a lot of unrest, the Vietcong were on the outskirts of town, and we were aware of battles as we stood on our roof watching the light-up flares in the area each night. They showed where the enemy was camped out. The American military was very visible, and every noon hour, the chaplain would bring them to us and hope for lunch! I'd come in from teaching at the American school and find them sprawled out on our terrazzo floors (no air conditioning). The chaplain could always count on fresh hot cinnamon buns! One big sergeant ate a dozen and finally got around to eating the lunch I had prepared! There was a week or two I couldn't find any flour anywhere, so no buns! The chaplain said he was tired of hearing this excuse all the time and got in his jeep and came back with three 50 lb. sacks of flour. He never told me where he got them. I had enough to share with my colleagues who were in the same predicament.

When the Tet Offensive hit, we heard the Vietcong were killing Americans in their homes at night. Since the Vietcong saw

American license plates on the cars in the driveway, they knew where to attack. Johnny took a felt pen, blackened out a paper, taped it over our license plate, and went to bed peacefully. The next morning there was paper strewn all over our driveway. Our dog had pulled it off, and here Johnny had slept so well. He was really upset with our dog! That day two of our MK graduates, Sam Meiss and Tim Zeimer, from our days of being in charge of the Dalat School, now Navy attaches, came to our gate to tell us to lay low and continued with frequent updates. One day we saw a whole truckload of American soldiers stop on our street. The kids ran out with lemonade and cookies. The guys were speechless, seeing these two blondes and a redhead.

The children and I did evacuate two days later when we got word from Johnny's Christian Children's Fund (CCF) director in Hong Kong to get the next flight out. The pilot didn't want to take the chance of being shot at, so he flew the plane straight up! CCF rented us an apartment high up on a cliff overlooking Deep Water Bay and enrolled the children at the International School. I was hired as a French teacher once again. During those two years, Johnny alternated between Hong Kong and Vietnam while he oversaw the 150 children's caseworkers, who were each responsible for 150 children.

Hong Kong had its eventful moments. One Sunday, missionary friends from Vietnam days, the Holtons, invited us to their home on an island at the Bible School. We took a ferry ride out there and enjoyed a Chinese meal with them. On our return, we got off the ferry at Wan Chai to catch a bus home. We saw a revolving barber sign, and I thought it would be a good idea while we were out for the boys to get a haircut. We walked up a long dark flight of stairs and finally came out on what looked like a barbershop.

There were girls standing around snickering. They made no effort to get the boys in a chair and just stood there. Finally, when Mark sat down, the girl went up the side of his head with clippers real close. I yelled out, "Do you even know what you're doing? Are you barbers?" We got up and left. The next day our CCF boss called and asked how our weekend had been. When I told him what happened, he said he was glad the place didn't get raided because the morning paper would have the headline, "CCF staff members getting haircuts for their sons in Wan Chai brothel!" We laughed over that experience. Poor Mark and Mel had to start school the next day with terrible haircuts. We had no idea we got off the ferry in the red light district.

Another time the Bollbacks were visiting us with their four children, and the kids were all playing kickball on the lower level of the apartment building with all its glass walls surrounding them. Judy, who was Donna's age, ran through the glass walls and severely cut her leg. Dr. Langford at Baptist Hospital saved her leg. Crisscross: Dr. Langford was working for a friend of Donna's in Lafayette years later when she and her son had to evacuate from New Orleans for Hurricane Katrina. When she saw Dr. Langford, she almost passed out. She remembered him also because he was the doctor that cleared me of cancer when I got my checkup years after he saved Judy's leg.

We attended the church where Tony Bollback was the pastor and loved it when we got included in the Chinese feasts after church. Crisscross: they were our neighbors in the retirement village we lived in Kissimmee, Florida. We enjoyed reminiscing when the kids would visit. The two oldest kids, Jim and Joy, attended Dalat as well, so it was always fun to see them. Judy and Donna have remained friends all these years. There's such a sense of family when we connected up years after our days in Vietnam with other missionaries and their kids.

Cleo Evans was also a neighbor and had been Donna's dorm mother in Dalat. She used to bring me my favorite bread every Tuesday when Publix donated their leftovers. Tim, who was one of our boys at Dalat and Cleo's son-in-law, used to visit Johnny every time he came to visit. We felt like he was a son and were so proud of him when he became a helicopter pilot, I even got to pin him with his mom, and later, he became Navy Admiral, then went on to serve in the White House as an advisor on Malaria.

When a storm hit, and we had to evacuate to a motel, which by the way Rick and Beth (Tim's sister) Drummond told us about, it only seemed natural to bring her along with us since Gene had passed and she was alone. We got adjoining rooms, and Donna joined us for a couple of days and stayed in the room with her auntie Cleo. She really liked that. When we went to check out after being there for two weeks, there was no charge. We were in shock. The owners told us since we had served their country all our lives—they were Vietnamese—they wanted to do something for us.

Tim Zeimer

Sam Meiss

Dalat

Chapter 12: Dalat School

"So don't be anxious about tomorrow. God will take care of your tomorrow too. Live one day at a time" (Matthew 6:34, TLB).

How crazy is it that I would return to Dalat School as the director's wife when I had attended there as a little girl? Nine months of the year, I attended Dalat School for missionary kids from all parts of South East Asia. After I spent three months with my parents, in order to get back to school from the most northern mission station, my dad would accompany me to the next railroad station, then return home. The next missionary with their child would take us to the next station where the same thing would happen. It was a three-day relay. I remember one time getting to Nhatrang, where there was no mission station (it was the last station before the train took us up the mountain). There were cots placed on the platform for us to sleep on. At one point, the missionary woke up and saw I was gone, only to find me sleepwalking on the tracks. I remember being brought back to my cot to spend the rest of the night. The train ride up the mountain was slow and tedious. So, we would get off and walk alongside the train. It was jungle on both sides. Our trips were adventurous.

At Dalat, I loved my dorm parents. Uncle Jackson always spoke to me in French, my mother's native tongue. I felt special when he called me *mon petit doux coeuer* (my little soft heart) or *mon petit choux choux* (my little cabbage head). Auntie's love was evident, even when she kept us in line. The Jacksons served at the tribes' center teaching at the Bible school when Johnny and I were assigned to Dalat School years later.

For a period of time, Johnny was asked to be director of the school when there was a lack of field personnel. Also, he was the chaplain for 150 children and for the local Army personnel. We were in charge of the boy's dorm as well and lived in the apartment in the corner of the L-shaped building so we could keep watch! We had seventy-five boys from first to twelfth grade whose missionary parents lived throughout Southeast Asia. I was an auntie to the boys and mom to my four-year-old Mark and baby Melvin. (Donna was in the girl's dorm and was allowed to visit on occasion.) I cared for the boys in the dorm as if they were my own. The younger ones, I tucked in at night after reading Bible stories to them and the next morning made sure they were all up with the rising bell. They had to keep their rooms clean and drawers neat. I made up fun chore contests with prizes to motivate them. The older boys had study hall at night, and when that ended, I had to make sure there were snacks, usually supper leftovers for those hungry guys.

I also had the fun job of taking kids on bike outings on Saturdays. We would go to the waterfalls, lake, or the mountains and have a picnic. I was the lead bicycler, and one of the older boys followed everyone at the rear. One time, a student had an accident that looked like it would require stitches. We took him to the local hospital. To my horror, I saw the doctor proceed as though he wasn't going to use anything to numb the area. I said, "What are you doing? You can't just stitch him up like that! You have to use this" (pointing to his cabinet with a bottle that indicated it was some type of local anesthesia). He consented to use the anesthesia because I was creating such a stir. The funny thing is I knew him well and didn't care if I would have to face him in the near future.

Our David lived at the far end of the hall with his classmates, and late at night, we'd find him sleepwalking, teeth chattering, and hands shaking. We'd get him back to bed. When our school doctor, Dr. Vietti, came for the yearly physicals, we checked him out with her. She said it was due to some traumatic experience. Then we realized we had been in Saigon at the guesthouse and were caught in the crossfire between the police department across the street and the Vietcong behind the house. There were nights we slept under our beds. When Johnny and David drove the Land Rover back to Dalat (Donna, Mark, and I flew back) en route, a bridge had been blown up, so they had to wait for a ferry and watch dead bodies floating by from a recent battle. David hadn't had a haircut for some months, nor had he clipped his nails. His teeth didn't seem to be growing, nor had his body! We sent a prayer request back to family and friends, and the Lord answered, and he began to grow normally again.

There would be nights our dogs would bark relentlessly only to hear our GI friends say they had been patrolling the woods around our buildings, knowing the VC was in the area. One day, a US Army lieut was very upset and came to our apartment looking for Johnny. Later, I found out he had just been in a battle and had to shoot into a group of women and children that the VC had placed in front of the village to protect those VCs that were hiding behind them. Johnny had a gift of showing compassion and the ability to stress the importance of turning pain over to God.

CHAPTER 13: BONDS WITH MANY INTERNATIONAL STUDENTS IN GAINESVILLE. OH, AND RUG MAKING AND WORMS

"But I will always trust in you and in your mercy and shall rejoice in your salvation. I will sing to the Lord because he has blessed me so richly" (Psalm 13:5–6, TLB).

When our furlough was approaching, we felt it would be good to pastor a church in the United States so we could be together as a family. David had just graduated in Malaysia with his classmates of twelve years. Dalat School had recently evacuated there from Vietnam.

The Gainesville C&MA church called my husband to pastor, and David decided to attend the University of Florida as he had been twelve years away from home in boarding school. We were pleased with his decision. Johnny, having the ability to see the needs in the community and the role the church could play in meeting the needs, opened a daycare center, making himself available to the parents early in the morning when they would drop off their children.

I got involved with international students on the campus of the University of Florida, and many began attending our church. Often on a Sunday, there would be as many as ten nations represented. Our parsonage was across the church parking lot, so it found many of them at our table at lunchtime. We never dreamed how far-reaching this influence on them could be. Years later, we got a call from a Vietnamese engineering student who'd been in our home in Gainesville and is now an engineer in Alaska. He was coming to Florida on vacation. He wanted to visit us with his wife, a lovely Dutch gal. (This past week, I spoke to them on FaceTime. They are now ministering in Vietnam in their retirement, self-supporting, exciting.) He found Jesus through her, and together, they were involved in their church. How thrilled we were to meet them and see what God had done in his life—not the most likely one from student days to follow Jesus. Later while pastoring in Montreal, one of our Gainesville couples, who were from Ghana, brought their baby to us for Johnny to dedicate to the Lord. Many students were sons and daughters of influential families. One such couple was Ted and Margaret Chen, who Johnny married. Margaret's dad flew a plane full of relatives from Taiwan over for the wedding. Hau and Minh Tam were another couple Johnny married and stayed good friends.

We still keep in touch with many of the students who attended the church and became family. Banke Ogenwalu keeps in touch through Facebook and so graciously calls me her mother. Her husband had a high government office before his passing a few years ago. We almost feel like we lost our own children when we said goodbye to several we knew we would not see again. One couple from Colombia tearfully said goodbye; we miss you, Oscar and Adiella.

People used to wonder how we could feed so many on our limited pastor's salary. I found a shed a few miles out in the country where farmers brought the produce in to be put on a conveyor belt where veggies with defects were thrown on the ground and left for grabs! I went early in the morning after the farmers left and brought back my loot, excited and ready to prepare it for the freezer. Another time one Saturday night, Melvin realized his rabbits needed food, so we drove to a produce stand and checked their garbage can! He found the lettuce, and I salvaged three cases of tomatoes that I took home and bagged for the freezer. Another time Mel was riding his bike around the neighborhood and found the dumpster in the back of the FritoLay factory—wow—was that a great haul with many future visits. God's provision!

Mel also raised worms for fishermen in the area and had a sign on the street, "Worms for Sale." It was a humbling experience for the pastor's wife when I'd get a knock at the door, and he wasn't home to go fill an order by digging worms out of the dirt box in the backyard.

Yet, when I found a dumpster that had strips and pieces of carpeting left over from a house being carpeted, I was so excited that I wasn't too proud to climb up and pull them out, even with heals on. The kids would lean down in the back seat, so embarrassed. I collected over a period of weeks until I had enough to mix and match and create a lovely carpet by gluing the strips on foam padding that I had taped together. This warmed up the parsonage's terrazzo floors. I met interesting people hanging over the dumpster and exchanging ideas—one young man told me he was carpeting his van.

A friend from Christian Women's Club came for a meeting and called me later asking me how a pastor's wife could afford an oriental rug. I laughed, telling her it had come from the dumpster! That took some explaining! Our international students also thought "rug gluing" enhanced their student apartments. Then some of the church ladies started getting creative as well.

Four years later, we were moved to Montreal. I collected more rejected carpeting, using it for padding when packing our moving van. This carpeting ended up completely carpeting a three-bedroom parsonage. The men in the church that unpacked our truck couldn't figure out what this new pastor's wife was up to with all the shag bits and pieces. A month later they were amazed at the finished product on our floors!

Chan wedding

Minh tam

Chapter 14: Montreal. Reaching out to Vietnamese Refugees; Cancer Strikes, God and I Strike Back

"Everyone shall stand in awe and confess the greatness of the miracles of God; at last they will realize what amazing things he does" (Psalm 64:9, TLB).

We had several good years in the Gainesville church, especially with international students. When the Dollard des Ormeaux (a suburb of Montreal, Quebec) church called us, they needed a couple who also spoke French. At that same time, close to 1000 Vietnamese refugees came sponsored by the Canadian government to Montreal. Our church reached out, and on Sundays, we'd have many come to our parsonage for dinner. Then the Ontario churches sent us truckloads of furniture and household goods. David and Mark took time off of college and grad school to distribute it, but the neighbors saw furniture being moved in and out of our garage. Later they told me that they thought I must be fickle, just having moved there, that the new pastor's wife couldn't make up her mind what she wanted!

The Russian church in Montreal had just built a new building and loaned us their old church for Vietnamese services and a warehouse for all the goods that came in from Ontario. The third floor was housing for our refugee pastor and family whom we had sponsored from being stuck in Korea when they escaped Vietnam, as it fell to Communism. I was recently speaking at a Vietnamese church in South Carolina, and a distinguished Vietnamese gentleman introduced himself. It was our former pastor from Montreal! What a nice surprise, with so many years of catching up to do!

I just found out he died this year of COVID-19.

It wasn't long after when I was diagnosed with invasive cancer, and even with radical surgery, chemotherapy, and radiation, the doctor couldn't give me hope! The morning we were headed to the hospital, my husband, Johnny, hugged me, and I felt extreme pain for the first time. I told him it felt like a vacuum cleaner suctioning up the invasiveness. The surgery showed the cancer was all encased in two ducts and that I would need a single instead of a double radical mastectomy. The nurse had one word in her vocabulary, "Amazing." During the months that followed, I had three other related surgeries, and I healed well and gave testimony to God's amazing power.

Within a matter of a couple of months, we were working eighteen hours a day in Hong Kong refugee camps.

Chapter 15: Hong Kong. CAMA, World Relief, and Tearfund England and Holland

"[…] Be strong and courageous and get to work. Don't be frightened by the size of the task, for the Lord my God is with you; he will not forsake you. He will see to it that everything is finished correctly" (1 Chronicles 28:20, TLB).

What is this verse trying to tell me when I'm sitting on my hospital bed waiting for my husband to take me home? "Get to work." Sure, I can do that. I am a caring pastor's wife and love being that. I'm not "frightened by the size of the task." I would have never dreamed my task would be working in Hong Kong with thousands of Vietnamese refugees just a month later under CAMA Services, the relief arm of the C&MA. World Relief later took us on due to the "size of the task," with other organizations like Tearfund England and Holland stepping in to fund projects. The work that could have been overwhelming became a joint effort, and we sensed God's presence as He continuously provided ways to meet the great need we encountered daily.

Many of the refugees came from areas we had served in the past twenty years. Others escaped from North Vietnam, where I had been raised in a C&MA missionary's home. I rejoiced in my heritage because I could relate in so many ways, especially with my language skills that I learned as a child but later had to study so I could preach and teach. They were amazed that a white person was speaking their language. I explained all this and that I had also studied Vietnamese eight hours a day for two years, so I could do just that.

Years later, I was in Saigon when Johnny and I were going in and out as we were no longer allowed to live there under the Communist regime. We were meeting with the head of the church. A former Vietnamese pastor now with World Vision was also in the room. I found out it was his dad that my dad was working with in Cao Bang up on the China border and where, as a kid, I would stay in their apartment above the church! Amazing! I was just a child at the time, a few years older than him. Later in California, I met up with his elderly mom, Mrs. Ba, who had taken me in as her very own—what a moving experience! She told me how she'd walk several miles across the border into China where she could buy a chicken cheaper, as she wanted one thing special to prepare for us, and they didn't have the money for that kind of purchase.

CHAPTER 16: FEEDING THE HUNGRY

> Feed the hungry, and help those in trouble. Then your
> light will shine out from the darkness, and the dark-
> ness around you will be as bright as noon. The Lord
> will guide you continually, giving you water when
> you are dry and restoring your strength. You will be a
> well-watered garden, like an ever-flowing spring.

> Isaiah 58:10–11 (NLT)

These are my favorite verses! The first time I had pondered these
words was when God brought them to my attention as I was waiting
to leave the hospital after a month and four surgeries. "Feed the
hungry." I have done this throughout history. In Dalat School for
several years, I oversaw the kitchen with a great cook who was the
cook thirty years before when I was a student. When I needed to
get on his case, he'd remind me, "Remember, you were just a little
girl here!" We had 150 hungry MKs, and they loved the food. Our
GIs would often pop in for home-cooked meals.

One time, GIs were coming in from a jungle base for Christmas, and I had been cooking for several days, but the day before,
I still didn't have my turkey. I wasn't willing for my helper to get
a hen in the local market because I knew it would be tough! That

day there was a knock at the door, a GI had two big turkeys in his arms, and my response was, "Wow! They must've dropped from heaven!" His reply was, "Yes, they did. The Saigon commissary airdropped us two shipments by mistake." Praise the Lord! There was my turkey and one for Cleo Evans, who was cooking in the next building for another large group.

In Gainesville, Florida, I had many hungry students after church each Sunday. In Hong Kong, Vietnamese refugees came ashore daily (120,000 in those three years) hungry from being lost at sea. Some were desperate. I met two girls in the camp clinic. They were comatose, and it wasn't until a few days later that they could tell me how there were twenty in their boat when they left Vietnam, and there was food to start out with, but after a few weeks… none! People started dying off, and as they did, they would tell the others to eat their vital parts. These girls felt terrible guilt, especially when they met up with relatives from their fellow travelers. A doctor said they couldn't possibly live with what they had been through. I prayed with them daily. They responded to love and God's forgiveness! It wasn't long before they attended our Bible studies and found the Lord. Their whole countenance changed, and their hollow eyes were bright again. Jesus made a difference.

We fed the hungry. However, the government did feed thousands of refugees at noon each day. They'd roll in large barrels, one with rice and the other with a thick soup. By the next morning, the children were crying from hunger. We got permission to give them special nourishing crackers from a Holland donation, and we ordered individual cartons of milk that the company had supplemented with extra vitamins.

When we worked for Franklin Graham in Croatia with refugees from Bosnia who had been raped and lost their homes and villages in the Serb conflict, some hadn't eaten for days. These pregnant women lived in our home for months on end and were always starving. I've never cooked such large pots of potatoes, and our nurse kneaded nourishing bread daily, for which they were so happy. It gave us joy to feed their relatives too, who just happened to appear at our door at mealtime. We got our food supplies from our SP warehouse, where trucks came in from England, Germany, Holland, and other European countries. I loved "shopping," not pushing a grocery cart but a hospital bed piled high with cases of interesting foods! Cooking was a challenge because I had to use what we had, so it required creativity with the supplies we got. One time we received many cases of baby formula, and since the girls breastfed their babies, I got the inspiration to make hot chocolate with it so it wouldn't go to waste. I made this for the girls nightly while they watched their TV show at 6:30. They couldn't tell the difference until Danica caught me one night and exclaimed, "Oh, Esther!"

One time a truckload from Germany arrived at the warehouse full of cabbages. Our nurse was so excited and got busy cutting them into eights and putting them in plastic garbage cans with brine to be soaked for days. I had forgotten about them until, one day, I was on the third floor, our dorm room, and smelled a terrible odor. Thinking it was next door and perhaps a couple of babies needed a diaper change, I started trying to follow the odor. The girls started giggling, knowing what I was trying to figure out. When I went down to the second floor, the smell got worse. Finally, I ended up in the basement garage only to find the cabbages. They were ready to eat as salad, and to the women's delight, we had months of this delicacy.

We had sixty-four women living with us during a two-and-a-half-year period with sixty-five babies born, including a set of twins. When we helped them reunite with their families, we gave them cases of basic foods to take back with them along with blankets, baby clothes in all sizes for their growing babies, and other essentials.

Chapter 17: Belarus and Romania

While we were serving in Croatia, Franklin sent us over to Belarus to encourage his staff, which was working in a difficult situation. We had our passports in hand but no visas as we were told they wouldn't be needed. We spent the next couple of hours locked in a stark, white room while the local Samaritan's Purse (SP) representative interceded for us at immigration. We had a lot of time to pray and think. We were finally released and enjoyed a cup of coffee at the bleak Communist hotel.

Belarus was still recovering from the Chernobyl explosion of a chemical factory, and we saw the terrible effects it had on the children and babies in the hospitals and orphanages. Pregnant women feared giving birth to deformed babies. It was heartbreaking. The SP director was from Belarus and had such a compassionate heart when there were so many needs. We met his wife and parents and had coffee in their little garden that supplied their table food.

Some months later, I came across an article of a boy in Belarus who had received a gift shoebox and had been encouraged to take the discipling course "The Greatest Journey." The last morning, he was desperately trying to finish the course and say the prayer to accept Jesus. His mom was trying to get him out the door to get to the church for the closing session when the explosion took place. He was one of the many that died in that terrible disaster, but he had Jesus in his heart.

After heart-wrenching moments in Belarus, we went on to Romania to spend time with the staff that was building a children's home on the Black Sea. The needs were great as hospitals were crowded with children suffering from serious conditions of AIDS. In their spare time, they spent time in the hospitals and crowded orphanages, holding and playing with children at death's door. We joined them along with the US Navy men whose fleet had docked in the harbor on one of their regular stops. It was very moving to see the response of the children as they felt so much love from the guys. Some of the men pitched in to help SP build the home where the sick children would get better care in their final days.

Seeing the poverty in Romania was heartbreaking. The market places even lacked produce. Your heart went out to see someone buying one carrot or a potato. The gypsies were everywhere, with Christian groups ministering to their physical and spiritual needs.

Chapter 18: Distribution of Love Buckets in Hong Kong

"Feed the hungry and help those [the thousands] in trouble" (Isaiah 58:10, NLT).

My very first moment in a tight security camp was heart-warming. After meeting the security officials, a girl with a baby walked over and squeezed a rolled paper through the window that was barely cracked open. I quickly got back in my car and took off as we weren't allowed to take communication out of the camp. When I read her note, she was asking me to find her husband, who had arrived in Hong Kong a year before her. My search took me to six camps with over 1,000 in each area. I would use the loudspeaker and call their names. At the last camp, a young man came running up. I told him about his sweet wife and cute baby he hadn't seen. He said he left ahead of her in Vietnam, hoping that one of them would be able to make it to safety when she followed, as so many little boats would go down at sea. He was able to get communication to her as he had made it to Hong Kong, but she didn't know which camp he was in. I took him over to the camp she was in for that special reunion. On the way, he told me he had a construction job, but because it was raining that day, he was there and heard his name come over the loudspeaker. They started coming to our center and heard of God's love for them through Jesus, which they just experienced and accepted Jesus as Savior, and grew spiritually the year and a half they remained in Hong Kong as they were being discipled. Finally, they got papers to be settled in England. A year later, we met up with them there.

The needs were great and ongoing in Hong Kong as refugees came ashore. Johnny created the "Love Bucket Project," giving each person a medium-size bucket with salt, sugar, toilet paper, soap, and a pair of rubber thongs, etc., including Vietnamese Christian literature. The bucket was used to collect their rice and soup at each meal or for however it was needed.

I have vivid memories of those who arrived in Hong Kong on little boats with not even a shirt on their back, so we supplied thousands of shirts and other items of clothing from the factories. Then when it got cold, we supplied ski jackets for a few dollars each due to minor flaws that kept them from being exported. The factory above the store threw hundreds out of their third store factory window down to the sidewalk below, and the owner packed my car. On arrival at the refugee camp, the kids swarmed me, stealing the jackets. As I threw myself on the jackets in the back of the van, I yelled, "Don't your parents teach you manners?" With that, they threw down their stolen goods and ran. What happened? I use the word *cha me*, meaning "mother and father," and a friend said I was cussing their ancestor's parents by using that term!

I enjoyed refuge work so much! Many times, Johnny had to step out in faith when he put in large orders for clothing and other necessary items for the love buckets from the Communist department store that offered him the best discounts. The funds always arrived in time when the truckloads came in.

It was overwhelming to see the thousands of refugees flowing into Hong Kong, a real challenge to the government to house everyone, much less to feed them. We felt led to help with those lodged in two tall buildings of ten floors. As we went from floor to floor to talk to the people, we saw we needed to open a clinic as the needs were so great, and there was available space on the ground floor. We hired a Chinese doctor that had just escaped China by swimming the Hong Kong harbor to safety. She was glad to have work. She couldn't speak English, but she could say, "Oh yes, yes." Then we hired a refugee doctor.

At one point, I had to go to the States, and on my last day in Hong Kong, I went from one bunk to another, talking with the refugees as this was their "home." I came to a mom and her eight-year-old son. She told me how her family of six were in a boat of twenty-eight, and just as they were being rescued, a big wave rammed them against the side of the ship, and everyone drowned except her and her son.

Fast forward, we were visiting Sam and Mary Vause in Greenville, South Carolina, a year later. They wanted to eat in a Vietnamese restaurant but were not sure how the food was. I volunteered to check it out! I asked the young man at the counter if the cook was Vietnamese, and he said, "Yes, my mom." As she stuck her head out of the kitchen, there was the mom and her son I had visited on my last day in Hong Kong. They lived down the street from Debbie Sofield's home, where we were staying. The next day they invited us for lunch and to meet the mom's brother, a Catholic priest who had gotten her sponsorship to the US. We had such sweet fellowship over lunch and prayed together. But God!

Chapter 19: Hong Kong Refugees and Friends in Canada

"When you obey me you are living in my love, just as I obey my Father and live in his love. I have told you this so that you will be filled with my joy. Yes, your cup of joy will overflow" (John 15:10–11, TLB).

There were volunteer medical people among the refugees, and one was a doctor, Dr. Bui Hong, with a wife and four children as well as his extended family members. They escaped Vietnam when the youngest was just a baby, and they called her Esther. Today she is an outstanding neurologist. Their boat was so packed Mrs. Hong didn't have space to even lay down. Now they were in the camp, and they had cardboard or mats. Every floor was literally wall-to-wall people. Their mat was their home, no privacy.

We invited people to a chapel we opened and used for Chinese and Vietnamese services. We had gospel literature printed in Vietnamese, and the people were so glad to have something to read. The Hong family came to the chapel, heard the good news of Jesus, and accepted Him as Savior. They were a lighthouse in a dark place. Dr. Hong helped many, right from his "home" on the floor. We found one family with a new baby that found refuge on a landing between floors. Their family ranged from a newborn to seventy-year-old grandparents. In talking to them, we had such joy as we found out that my dad had led the "patriarch" to the Lord in North Vietnam sixty years prior.

To get their food, some had to walk the ten floors with the "love buckets" we had given them. Gradually they were moved to camps less crowded and could get jobs in many factories in Hong Kong. Our doctor friend babysat and took care of the sick while his wife went out to work. Instead of mats, the Hong family graduated and had a three-layered wooden bunkbed with three to a bed and hundreds all around them in the room. Every time we came to visit, they were joyful and hospitable, and we always found them caring for the sick.

A church in Ontario, Canada, said they would sponsor the Hongs. So, I connected them with Canadian immigration officials. Due to complications, it took a couple of years for clearance. In the meantime, they were active in our Vietnamese church, the second floor of a building that Tearfund England bought for this ministry. This center daily met the needs of the refugees with varied activities. The Hong family was finally on their way to Owen Sound, Canada. With much hard work and sacrifice through the following years, all three boys and their daughter became doctors. Luke is a surgeon and chief of staff at two hospitals, and Esther is a neurologist who is deeply committed to helping women with epilepsy and is also cross-appointed to the Division of Obstetrical Medicine. When I visited her at the hospital, I was deeply moved by her commitment to women with neurological conditions. She even finds time to teach at the University of Toronto as a clinician-educator. San is a chiropractor and runs four rehab clinics. Mark is an acupuncturist and also has a land development business.

Last year the Hongs invited me to their fiftieth wedding anniversary to pray in Vietnamese and share at their big reception with over 150 guests. It was a delicious twelve-course Chinese meal. The four children honored their parents with touching speeches of their appreciation for where they are today and especially that they know Jesus and how it all began in Hong Kong with their mom and us. I had three precious weeks as a guest of the Hongs and their children in Toronto, such beautiful Christians.

Hongs

For the next three weeks, I was in Calgary, Alberta, for Vietnamese ministry, where Johnny started a Vietnamese church within First Alliance Church, where he served as administrative pastor. Lanh assisted him in the services. His grandfather was head cook at Dalat School, and his father was our baker when we were at the school in Dalat. We had the privilege of being with those we led to Jesus in Hong Kong. It was so good to see Mr. Bau, who would every Monday night distribute goods with me to the refugees coming into Calgary under government sponsorship. They let me know they had arrived since they didn't have personal contact with anybody. Mr. Bau's son, Huy, used to come over and sit with Johnny when we would house-sit for our friends, the Zielstras, who were on vacation in Holland and so generously gave us the chance to get out of our apartment and enjoy their beautiful home on a lake. Huy still quotes some of Johnny's humorous insights. I know Johnny enjoyed Huy's company. The only wedding ceremony Johnny ever performed in Vietnamese was for Huys's brother, Tung. Huy still keeps in close contact with me by phone.

Huy reminded me of the first time he saw me at the refugee camp when he was a little boy. He had Donna laughing so hard when he told her I had an army green dress on. She asked him how he remembered the color, and he said at first he heard the click, click, click of high heels tapping across the cement floor, but it was hearing this tall white lady speaking his language to the short refugee camp director that left him with such a powerful memory. He couldn't wrap his head around a white lady speaking Vietnamese. He said it was the way I was talking to him, with such authority, like I knew what I was doing! This had both Donna and me in stitches.

We had dear friends at First Alliance in Calgary since Johnny was on staff there. We met the Loewens first in their travels in Hong Kong. Then the Holters were heavily involved with the Vietnamese, and we got close through that ministry. We first met the Hargreaves when their boys were toddlers, and they have children of their own now. Bill and Cheryl have been like family through the years. The same goes for the John Claytons. Our friendship began in Croatia, where John was our boss. He works for SP Canada. He lovingly calls me his mom and is consistently humble when I introduce him as my former boss.

Bui

Chapter 20: Dolphin Guided Safety

"There before me lies the mighty ocean, teeming with life of every kind, both great and small. And look! See the ships! And over there the whale you made to play in the sea" (Psalm 104:25–26, TLB).

A boat of seven young men came ashore late one evening, and we helped them with a late supper and gave them clothes as theirs had rotted off their backs at sea from the water, salt, and sun. What a thrill to hear their story of how "the man of the heaven" had used two dolphins to lead them to safety and how they said they'd follow God if they were ever rescued. They were tossed around at sea when the dolphins appeared in front of their boat as they saw a ship off in the distance. Excitedly, they tried to head in that direction, but the dolphins got in their way, pushing them in a different direction. An hour later, the dolphins were gone. They met up with the ship and were picked up. They realized if they had kept going in their original direction, this wouldn't have happened. They all attended a Bible study at the center and found the Lord!

The Vietnamese Refugee Center came about as a result of one Sunday when we attended the English-speaking church in Hong Kong. At the close of the service, on the front steps, we met two British gentlemen who told us they had come from Tearfund

England, intending to help the Vietnamese refugees, but *how*? A miracle! We told them of our need for a Vietnamese center for worship and to disciple those that were coming to the Lord. We spent the rest of Sunday taking them to the refugee camps to see their needs. Within days they sent us the money to purchase the third floor in a building accessible to one of the camps. They also sent funds to buy clothing for new arrivals. Johnny got an old double-decker bus from the city and, with their funds, remodeled the bus and set up a typing school for the refugees needing a vocation when processed to a third country.

Typing school in an old school
bus TearFund bought

We brought a Vietnamese couple, Rev. and Mrs. Tot, to pastor the church and evangelize in the camps. Johnny also sent me and a friend, Marni Mock, to the Philippines to minister, where there were thousands of Vietnamese, Cambodian, and Lao refugees in the Bataan refugee camp. Larry Ward, with Food for the Hungry, paid their way from the States to Hong Kong. There were open-air evangelistic nightly meetings, movies shown (*Life of Christ* in Vietnamese), and sharing Jesus door-to-door as well as staff to minister to the many children. Amongst them was our future daughter-in-law, Chris, who always had an entourage of little children following her around. They loved her! She looked like the pied piper with all these children following her so closely.

Chapter 21: Cooking School in Hanoi

"[…] Then your light will shine in the darkness, and the darkness around you shall be as bright as noon" (Isaiah 58:10b, NLT).

"God is the LORD, which hath shewed us light" (Psalm 118:27a, KJV).

"The LORD is my light and my salvation—whom shall I fear?" (Psalm 27:1a, NIV)

As you obey God, feed the hungry, and help those in need, the above becomes a reality. Jesus is the light of the world, and when we accept Him as Lord and Savior, He dwells within us. His light permeates us.

The first time I experienced this was when I walked into a crowded warehouse with wall-to-wall people and met some of their needs. We had outdoor meetings each night in the camps, and again, I let them know I appreciated my heritage so I could communicate Jesus to them in their language. A group of professional Vietnamese musicians joined in performance each night. They had traveled all over Eastern Europe, performing their Communist government propaganda. They escaped Vietnam and accepted Jesus in our meetings, and joined us, performing for Jesus. Several years later, one of them, John Pham, was hired by Samaritan's Purse to be (country) director in North Vietnam to start many projects to help his own people and share Jesus.

When I first met John Pham in Hong Kong, he had just arrived on the dock, and he asked me if I knew Ruth Wilting. I told him she had been our school nurse when Johnny was director of the Dalat Missionary Kids School. He said he came to the school each week as a university student to study English with Ruth using the Bible. Then I remembered I had met him on several occasions. His father called him back north to Hanoi as Vietnam was being divided, and now all these years later, our paths crossed again in Hong Kong.

He told me he wanted someday to be helping us in Vietnam! I told him I doubted we'd ever be given permission to work in Vietnam under the Communist regime. On one of our trips to Vietnam, can you guess who the Vietnam Samaritan's Purse Director was? John Pham! We worked under him for those days. That's what missions is all about. It gave us such joy to feel his heart for his people during our visit. John picked up two boys one night in a park in Hanoi, cold and hungry, and later adopted them to join his son Mark who he brought out of Viet Nam. His wife died of cancer before he fled the country as a refugee. One of the boys served in a tribal area on the China border until he went to seminary in the Philippines. The other one went to a cooking school that Samaritan's Purse helped to support, and he now has a restaurant in Saigon.

Recently, Franklin had four students from the school come to Boone and asked me to go up and come alongside them for a couple of months as they enhanced their cooking skills in our SP kitchen. They won the hearts of the several hundred staff members that ate in the SP dining room. They also felt the Christian love shown them during those months and came to understand more about Jesus.

Chapter 22: An Ever-Flowing Spring

"[…] and you will be like a well-watered garden, like an ever-flowing spring."

"[…] and satisfy you with all good things, and keep you healthy too; and you will be like a well-watered garden, like an ever-flowing spring" (Isaiah 58:11, TLB).

What a powerful verse this was to me as I meditated on it in the hospital in Montreal after four weeks and waiting to go home. I obeyed God's commands, and that became a reality in the months that followed in Hong Kong and the Philippines, that He would satisfy me. I had no greater pleasure than to meet the refugees' needs, my Vietnamese people, and He'd keep me healthy after just getting over four surgeries in four weeks.

Johnny and I had the privilege at one point of being guests of Tearfund England and sharing the work in Hong Kong. They had us stopping in Israel en route back to Hong Kong. In Jerusalem, we were booked in a monastery, with no heat and so cold we hardly got out from under the covers, but when we did, we walked the streets of Jerusalem where Jesus walked. Johnny enjoyed a special treat, often stopping to get a scoop of special couscous pudding cooking in a large pan over an open fire. Yum! It also heated our bones in the bitterly cold weather. While in Jericho, while we were on a hill overlooking the desert, our driver saw our gaze on a patch of green. He told us there was an ever-flowing spring of water there, and I had the visual of my favorite verse that with His Holy Spirit flowing through us, we bring life to those about us.

Chapter 23: Preordained Meeting of a Nun Under an Umbrella

"Many are the plans of man, but it is the purpose of the Lord that will stand" (Proverbs 19:21, ESV).

One day while working in Hong Kong, not only was our World Relief boss coming to town but a British official from an organization sponsoring some of our projects. Johnny told me I was to escort the gentleman from England, but he needed the Honda, and that was the car I always drove. The other vehicles were on that day already in use. I, of course, was upset and complaining but knew this was displeasing to God. I headed out but forgot my umbrella in the car that had driven me to the bus area. I picked up my distinguished British guest, and he was fine about walking in the rain as he wanted to see our activities in the camp that he was sponsoring. At the end of that morning, I felt like a drowned rat but had to take him (and me) to meet Johnny and our boss for lunch. We were standing at the bus stop. There was a Catholic nun under her umbrella, and I prayed she would be kind and offer to share it with me. And she did! I asked her if she knew "Sister Emma." She said, "Yes, she's my roommate." An absolute miracle! I had been looking for this nun for weeks, calling every Catholic establishment with no success. The reason for my search was that a recent Vietnamese refugee arrival in Hong Kong had asked me to find her two children who were somewhere in the world! She had put them on a boat in Vietnam. There was no room for her, but anxious for their safety, she figured they'd meet up somehow. She got to Hong Kong, finally, a year later and found out that a sister Emma had befriended her two children and gotten them sponsorship to Germany. She knew the sister had been corresponding with them. I had been searching for over a month, and because of the umbrella, I had such good news for my despairing Vietnamese mother. I shared all this with my British friend on the bus, and he was truly moved and amazed. I had to confess how I had mumbled and complained about not having use of the little Honda that day. Johnny and our boss were moved as I shared my story over lunch. This was a special lesson to me in my work with the Lord of obedience to my husband, much less complaining and being upset with not getting my way.

Philippians 2:14 (TLB) says, "Stay away from complaining if you want to shine out in a dark world for Jesus" (paraphrased). As I think of obedience, if He is Lord, our only option is to do His will and let Him be in control. Our lives are drastically changed by our choices.

Chapter 24: We Meet Again in Finland

"For to be sure, he was crucified in weakness, yet he lives by God's power. Likewise, we are weak in him, yet by God's power we will live with him in our dealing with you" (2 Corinthians 13:4, NIV).

"With Jesus' help we will continually offer our sacrifices of praise to God by telling others of the glory of his name" (Hebrews 13:15, TLB).

We were back in Geneva, Switzerland, under Food for the Hungry, where Johnny was vice president of their international office. We had made such good friends at the English-speaking church, and I was involved with the Christian Women's Club (CWC), an outreach to women over a luncheon held monthly. This one day, I was walking along the park by Lake Geneva, going over my message for CWC. I was heavy-hearted while thinking of the message I was to give as I had just gotten a disturbing message from one of my children back in the United States. *How was I to share Jesus feeling like I did?* Then the verse came to me that I had to offer the Lord praise, and it wasn't going to be easy, and it would have to be a sacrifice that would only come with Jesus' help as I gave testimony to the women the next day. I struggled as I walked, looking at God's wonderful creation. I was praying, shedding a few tears, but with His power, I was able to speak the next day. A "sacrifice of praise" has meant a lot to me through the years as we have faced difficult circumstances.

"Why, my soul, are you downcast? Why so disturbed within me? Put your hope in God, for I will yet praise him, my Savior and my God" (Psalm 42:5, NIV).

Food for the Hungry International's office (FHI) in Geneva at the time was very small and inadequate. One Sunday, we were driving home from church to our apartment in Versoix. We passed by two big Napoleon Bonaparte homes, and Johnny said, "I believe God is going to give us one for an office." I said, "What? You have to be kidding. It would be out of our financial range." But God! Next morning at 6:30, our Swiss pastor friend, a childhood friend of my mother, called and said the owner of the two homes called to ask him if he knew of anyone in need of a house. She explained that the Moonies had been renting and now were giving it up, and she wanted Christians in there to counteract the heathen worship of the Mooney organization. We went right over and were amazed at the huge rooms and wide lawn between the house and Lake Geneva. We got our pastor friend and his assistant to walk with us from the basement to the attic to pray over and cleanse each room from satanic activities. What praise went up to the Lord for His goodness.

FHI and our lawyer were working on our visas, and until they were in hand, we had to be gone for the weekend. If the police came to our apartment and found we didn't have a visa, they could demand we leave the country immediately. So FHI bought us a three-month Eurail Pass, and how we enjoyed traveling all over Europe each weekend during the three months before our work permit came through. That was no "sacrifice of praise."

One Friday, Johnny met me at the Geneva train station and asked where we were going as he knew I had worked out some itinerary. Since it was a holiday on Monday, I had planned a longer trip up into Scandinavia, hoping we could meet up with some Vietnamese refugees that were resettled there. Since I hadn't heard back from them, it was a step of faith. As we settled in our compartment, I told Johnny that the first night we should be in Copenhagen, Denmark, and the next morning on to Sweden and catch the ferry that next day on to Finland. "Oh!" Johnny said as he pulled out a letter from his jacket. And guess what it was? It was a letter from one of the young men in Hong Kong that had been my right arm. Every week he'd help me take fifty refugee children to the Suen Dough camp for the day of recreation, food, and Christian teaching, a great way to share God's Word with them. When we got to Finland, we called him, he was so excited, and within fifteen minutes, he was meeting us at the train station and taking us back to his apartment.

He was so pleased that we could meet some of the refugees that met with him for Bible study each week. To our amazement came a young man in his wheelchair who just about jumped out of his skin! Our Mark had bought him that wheelchair in Hong Kong with his own money. I remembered the day that Mark lifted him up into the wheelchair, saying, "He has crawled on the ground long enough, twenty-five years, and needs to feel some dignity for a change."

What a happy evening being with our friend who found the Lord in Hong Kong and now, in turn, was reaching out to his fellow Vietnamese. The power of the gospel was keenly felt as they shared with us what God was doing in their lives, despite the fact they had hoped to be resettled in the US.

Chapter 25: Plastic Surgeries, Trach Tube, and IV Bag

"But for you who revere my name, the sun of righteousness will rise with healing in its rays. And you will go out and frolic like well-fed calves" (Malachi 4:2, NIV).

We had the privilege of accompanying a medical team of doctors and nurses to Nha Trang, where they performed hair lip surgeries. The lines were long of children to be examined. When the children finally were in the next line, they were so excited they'd run down the hall to the operating room with their examining robes flying open behind them and then jumping up on the surgery table. They had seen the results of previous surgeries and were thrilled to think they would no longer be mocked and laughed at with their grotesque-looking lips. Periodically, I would go to recovery and see how the children and ER nurses were doing and interpret where needed.

One day, I saw this very large American man unconscious on the operating table. I was told he'd been in a serious motorcycle accident and needed surgery. The doctors needed a large-size trach tube that they were waiting for a flight from Saigon to bring them, but when? Then I remembered when we left Greenville, South

Carolina, to come on this trip, a doctor friend gave us a suitcase full of medical supplies that I didn't have a clue what they were for! We rushed back to our hotel room and brought back what looked like a trach tube. When the doctor saw what we had, he was almost moved to tears. It was the exact size he needed to save this big man's life. His mom flew in from the US and was so grateful.

Two weeks of day-long surgeries did not end the lines of waiting moms with their disappointed children. It was heartbreaking to see but hopeful in the future more doctors would volunteer to serve. One of our surgeons returned some months later. Johnny couldn't accompany him as he was having five bypass surgery.

While doctors were doing the hair lip surgeries, the orthopedic surgeon was busy too. A forty-year-old girl who had been crawling on the ground all those years in the dust and dirt and mud was lifted up. Her dignity as a person was restored. Our doctors followed Christ's example of healing physical suffering so the patients could understand the message of the love of Jesus.

On that same trip to Nha Trang, we had an overnight in Saigon. Late that night, there was a loud knocking at our door. It was a dear pastor friend and his wife. She was crying, and he was ashen. They told us how they had been to every pharmacy in town looking for a bag of IV glucose. Their sixteen-year-old daughter was in the hospital after trying to take her life because her dad was not allowing her to marry the guy she loved! The doctor didn't have this IV available at his hospital and sent the parents out on a search only to find no glucose available anywhere in the city. I remembered while I was in SC, I wanted to pack this bag of liquid in our suitcase, but Johnny had been very reluctant to pack it in our bag. I insisted, as our doctor friend who had given it to us had said we just might need it! But God!

Daily over coffee, we interpreted for our surgeons and the Vietnamese doctors. They shared stories of the war years in Vietnam when the local Vietcong doctors would be trying to do surgery in the jungle, and they'd hear American bomber planes close by. They would have to keep working while soldiers would be trying to move the surgery table to safety. They told our doctors how frightening that was! Our American doctors told them practically the same story! We were interpreting for both sides that had been enemies and now working together to bless little children. The doctors got up from both sides of the table and came around to hug each other. It was a very moving experience. Daily as we drank coffee with them, they would ask why the American doctors would give up time from their lucrative practices to help in this way. It was a great opportunity to share Jesus and His love for little children.

Chapter 26: Vietnam Director of Social Services Expresses Interest in Joining CAMA Services

"When you obey me, you are living in my love, […] so that you will be fulfilled with my joy. Yes, your cup of joy will overflow" (John 15:10–11, TLB).

On several of the trips to Vietnam, we met with the director of social services, and he would take us to visit orphanages and other projects they needed help with. At one meeting, he informed us that when he retired that year, he wanted to join CAMA Services! All we could say was, "That's interesting." We didn't know what else to say. Here was a Communist leader saying he wanted to join CAMA Services. He went on to say, "You all are so happy, and I want to tell you a Bible story." A Bible story from a Communist leader? This should be really interesting. Even though it may not be a story in your Bible, it proved to be an excellent story about these people who were at a banquet table and couldn't pick up their food and put it in their mouths because their chopsticks were too long. The food sat before them, and they couldn't enjoy it.

Finally, someone got the notion to feed the person across the table from them, and they were happy because they could help each other, they could serve each other! He said, "This is what you do when you come to Ho Chi Minh City, better known to you as Saigon." He said, "You help us to help our people because they are so needy, and we as a country are desperately needing help." We said we needed to be friends, and he thanked us for our ongoing help with the disabled children's institutions. He said, "There is happiness in helping others, and you seem to be so happy."

Yes, there is joy in serving God. God has called us to be happy people because we are privileged people. We are privileged to be God's children because of what God did in sending His Son to die so that we might have forgiveness of sins and become part of His Family.

Chapter 27: Vietnamese Professionals Give Back

"The light of the eyes rejoiceth the heart: and a good report maketh the bones fat" (Proverbs 15:30, KJV).

One of CAMA's projects is to help the church help its own people in providing the money for people to go to distant villages where there is a church and where there hasn't been any help for years.

One Sunday night, a bright-eyed, joyful, happy little Vietnamese lady came to me after the service in the Saigon church. She was so excited because she was having the opportunity to reach out in love and serve her Lord by helping her own very poor and needy people.

A Chinese Christian businessman rents a van, and professional people donate their time and talent to help their own people, reaching out in love in action as well as sharing their faith in Jesus. The average person makes $12 to $20 a month, and they don't have the funds to work with. These people are so poor they can't even afford a haircut. So, a barber joined the group and became a channel of love as he ministers.

The bright-eyed, joyful little lady at church was a dentist. The first month she pulled eighty teeth. The next month another lady dentist joined her, and the count was one hundred and twenty. She said the second month was such hard work even though there were two of them as it might be the people in the village have a different diet, the first month was so easy. What a sweetheart! Her light was shining out in a dark place because she was helping those in need. Can you imagine the impact that team had in that village and how it strengthened the testimony of the local evangelical church in the village? People were seeing love in action. The seventy-two-year-old pastor of the church in the village rode all day in the hot sun on his bicycle into Ho Chi Minh City to beg the leader of the team to come back with medical people and the barber as it had given the church such credibility in the eyes of the villagers.

The villagers saw compassion in action. The first month we were able to give them $100, and it bought enough medicine to take care of 600 patients that day. Money goes a long way. The next month with $250 worth of medicine, the team ministered to 1200 people, physically and spiritually as well.

CHAPTER 28: A SMILE IS A UNIVERSAL LANGUAGE

A smile, is it an unexpected token of God's love and care? When it comes at the perfect time, it may still troubled water.

"[…] I will forget my complaint, I will change my expression, and smile" (Job 9:27, NIV).

I was sitting in a small hotel waiting for someone to pick us up (and by the way, we were assigned to a hotel by government tourism when we arrived, and the hotels are much to be desired). We were to be picked up at 1:00, but they came at 5:00. There is an expression, rubber time—*Dong Ho Cao Shu*—it stretches. I watched the people go by. I felt frustrated. Our ministry was no longer preaching to the thousands in refugee camps in Hong Kong. Sometimes a ministry can be for a particular season. The crowd went by, and I couldn't even talk to anyone around me, much less preach. From month to month, the political atmosphere in the country would change depending on what was going on in China, Eastern Europe, the US, etc. This time we were told not even to speak Vietnamese because we were being watched and we needed an extension on our visa, and speaking Vietnamese might bring suspicion as to who we really were, and our motives for being in Vietnam might be questioned.

Frustrated, I picked up a book, and my bookmark was in a place about the subject, communication (words, touch, smile). I went out on the sidewalk as the crowds passed by and just made eye contact smiling. They'd almost wreck their bikes because they thought we were Russians, and Russians don't smile much!

While writing this and thinking about how effective non-verbal communication can be, I thought of the Miengs who had been through so much, even imprisonment but exuded such joy. Pastor Mieng was head of the C&MA church for many years.

I also thought Tri (the Ba Vinh story) was so full of joy when we talked on the phone recently. When he asked me to share Jesus with his in-laws, I thought they would already know he and his wife had an inexplicable joy as we shared on facetime, the kind of joy that comes from knowing Jesus on a personal level. He had already shared with them before I ever said anything by his very countenance.

Croatia

Chapter 29: Franklin Graham's Home for Women in Samobor, Croatia

"I can do everything God asks with the help of Christ who gives me the strength and power" (Philippians 4:13, TLB).

"The LORD is my strength and my shield; my heart trusted in Him, and I am helped; Therefore, my heart greatly rejoices, And with my song I will praise Him" (Psalm 28:7, NKJV).

"You will keep in perfect peace whose minds are steadfast, because they trust you" (Isaiah 26:3, NIV).

When Franklin Graham asked us to go to Croatia, we had just returned from living in Thailand and going in and out of Vietnam for special projects. We were already into our retirement years but felt blessed to think we could still be active in God's work. We were to run a home for women who were victims of the Serb conflict who'd been raped, needing a peaceful environment and loving "parents" to care for them. We accepted the challenge. There was always rumbling of the war in the distance, which Vietnam had prepared us for.

A nurse was on our full-time staff, and a lady doctor, also a Bosnian, gave us half days. She brought her daughter Amina from a refugee camp three hours away, where she was being threatened,

"Wait until you have your baby; we'll kill that little Serb." We bonded immediately. An hour later, she was left with us. She spoke a little English and told me how she had been in the concentration camp. Her dad was taken off, never to be seen again, and her boyfriend was killed. Red Cross got her, and she was reunited with her mom. Ten months prior, a Serb soldier took her from her home and raped her. She returned hours later, a basket case, no self-worth, and defiled. I talked with her, shared God's love with her, and read Psalm 139 to her. Things went well, but it was a traumatic hospital experience when it was time for her delivery; such hatred shown to her because she was carrying a Serb baby. She came back to our home thin, worn, depressed, and fearful. She lived with emotional trauma and was afraid everyone was going to kill her baby. She could hardly sit still for a meal because she was so worried someone was going to get her baby. She needed hours of counseling.

We used to sit around in the living room, and the girls would share their stories. One girl told us how the enemy soldiers attacked her village and came into their home and beheaded her dad right before her very eyes. Another girl used to sit on the balcony of our home with her boyfriend. He would put his arm around her in a protective manner. We learned they were separated in a concentration camp. The soldiers would come into the girl's dorm at night, and whoever their flashlight ended up shining on was taken out and raped. In the boy's dorm, the young man was taken out and killed.

Another girl's husband had been shot right in front of her, and when her mother-in-law heard the shots, she came out and saw her son lying in a pool of blood and died of a heart attack. She was eight months pregnant with twins at the time. There were too many stories like this to share.

One story I feel compelled to share is that of our translator, Emina, who had lost two babies to lung infection, and when she was pregnant again, the doctor offered her accommodations with us where she could be monitored since it would be very costly to stay in the hospital. Deep bonds were formed with the ten girls she shared a room with. Often in conversation, they would ask how they could get along so harmoniously and those outside could not. She soon found the answer was that only in Christ were forgiveness, reconciliation, and co-existence possible. She told me all of the women in the home experienced the truth of God's love through living side by side with Johnny and me, who daily affirmed this kind of love in practice. She said it was all of our love, care, service, patience, sacrifice, and kindness that spoke on behalf of our faith. It was Franklin's vision and provision through SP that made this possible, for which I am eternally grateful. It was her newfound faith and commitment to God that made her strong enough to face the next tragedy.

The tragedy occurred six months after giving birth to her son Robbie while returning to Bosnia. She and her husband had a car accident when they landed up in a river. Here is the story: "It was like we were in a movie. In shock and disbelief, we looked at each other, not understanding what had just happened. We devised a rescue plan. Robbie's cries and the cold water that was filling the inside of the car had brought us back to reality. I heard my husband telling me to go get Robbie, and after that, nothing more. All at once, all around me, there was water. I looked around me, but the water was very cloudy and, therefore, hard to see through. I remembered the seatbelt and unfastened it. In vain, I tried to find an exit. I was disoriented, and wherever I touched, it was closed. The pain in my lungs became unbearable. Death was very near: it was knocking on my door. And then, like a drowning man grasping for his last breath, in my thoughts, I began to feverishly address God, 'My God, is this my death? Will I really die? God, how can I die conscious and with a sound mind?'

"The last thing I remember was feeling the steering wheel under my arm, and then completely, unexpectedly, I began my journey to the surface. Hands extended high above my head; I came out of the water with the feeling that I had fallen from some altitude into it. Immediately I saw my husband holding onto a branch on the shore. When he looked at me, he screamed like he had seen a ghost. He kept repeating, 'I can't.'

"My body was broken and in pain. The water current carried me to him. Through tears, he told me how he tried to save Robbie, but the water pressure pushed him out the moment he opened the door. In desperation, he dove into the car seven times. However, great pain and the discovery that it was too late for his child drove him. Helplessly and desperately, we watched the headlights of our car in the depths of the blue Neretva River. Loudly and seemingly without end, we cried and asked God over and over, 'Why did you leave us alive? Why didn't we die altogether?'

"Two hours later, divers pulled our child out of the car. We were taken to the morgue. This was the last time we could touch and kiss our son's body. This time he was cold and lifeless. Thick, coarse black hair framed his chubby little cheeks. On one cheek was a bruise from the impact. Was his death painful?

"The funeral passed. We had to go on living because we couldn't live in the grave. Life was empty and painful, and many things reminded us of him. We couldn't change our apartment, furniture, and many other things to forget him. My husband demanded that we remove all of our son's photographs: he was deeply inconsolable. He blamed himself and suffered because he had lived and Robbie had died.

"I said we found ourselves at a crossroads, and God had given us a new opportunity to choose that which up now we didn't have, and that was God Himself and His blessings. Things developed differently for me. The Lord brought peace to my heart, which didn't seem normal to others. When people came to express their sympathy, I would quote the Bible to them, telling them that we are saved by faith in Jesus Christ and not by works, etc. They thought I had gone crazy, but there were those who left our home comforted. That wonderful seed that was planted in my life in Samaritan's Home was now bringing forth abundant fruit of comfort and healing. The Lord revealed His mercy to us bit by bit. Soon I got answers to all the questions that were bothering me. I brought God's supernatural comfort to my family and beyond.

"One morning, we were all sitting together. The situation was painful and difficult. Robert's mother cried and said she was leaving us because she blamed herself for all that had happened to us. At that moment, God gave me His strength and Word. I read Deuteronomy 30, which says that God puts before us a choice: life and happiness or death and unhappiness, blessings or curses. I said that we found ourselves at a crossroads and that God had given us an opportunity to choose that which we didn't have up until now, and that was God Himself and His blessings. We could try it out and take a chance. *What did we have to lose?* It was time to change our direction and our lives. Everyone was quiet and reflected on what I had said. I believed in the living, powerful Word of God, which never returns to God void.

"One day Robert asked me, 'Do you remember your miraculous escape from the water? I saw how you were pulled out from the water to where it was thigh high. It was a real miracle of God. Praise God through all the ages!' The Lord answered my cries with His miraculous redemption, which was my new start: new life in me and for me. In His tremendous mercy, He didn't want us to die because that would have meant eternal death. I understood that our children were in God's arms and that His love toward them was greater than our love. Also, He provided for both of us a way to eternity. That way was His Son, Jesus Christ.

"What would we have profited if all these things hadn't happened, and we didn't get to know the Lord, salvation, and eternal life? Just as it is written in the Word of God, 'For what will it profit a man if he gains the whole world, and loses his own soul?' (Mark 8:36, NKJV)

"How immeasurably merciful is our precious God! He is full of surprises and intensely desires to be glorified in our lives! He restored us spiritually and blessed us with children. We now have a son, John (Ivan) Daniel, and a girl, Tabitha.

"We are deeply grateful to the Lord for lively and healthy children and for being parents again. Let our Lord God be glorified and praised for all that He has done for us! Hallelujah! And still, this isn't the end of the story…"

Chapter 30: Two Bakers

"I am the vine; you are the branches…" (John 15:5a, NIV) Our home was high on a hill overlooking the town of Samobor, completely surrounded by vineyards, continually reminding us of our position in Christ as branches depending on the vine for our nourishment and strength.

I did most of the cooking in Samobor at our Women's Home with Seka, the nurse assisting with baking the bread each day. After she'd climbed the long hill to our home, she'd get out the big bowl to make her famous bread. By lunchtime, it had raised and was ready to be formed into one big square loaf that just fit into our small oven. (Our small stove had two burners.) The fragrant aroma of bread filled the house, making everyone eager to be called for lunch. We'd enjoy what was left for supper. I could never figure out why it was so difficult to slice through Seka's bread until, through translation, I found out in the warzone, if a house was left standing with a stove, neighbors would take turns and share the oven. To make the bread last for days, they would bake it a long time.

We could sleep ten women in a big dorm room on the third floor and two rooms when their babies came. We had two small automatic washers. When I wanted to murmur to myself that I didn't come to the mission field to do diapers, I remembered my years in Dalat School in Vietnam, where I thought I learned to be content and not complain when nightly I had to sort the clean socks that came from the laundry and try to match them for seventy-five boys. It's hard enough to match them for your husband, much less for that many boys! I was being tested again, often for a poor attitude!

One time I had baked my specialty carrot cake and had just enough left over to serve the girls a slice for teatime. Some Islamic doctors had come to visit one of our women. I wasn't sure of their motives, so I wasn't about to share my precious cake with them. Our nurse had fixed her strong coffee for them, and I got out some dry biscuits and was putting them on a plate when the Lord really convicted me of my attitude, and they did get my cake! Later as I was accompanying them to the door, their interpreter quietly said to me, "What is it about this home that is so different than the other Islamic-run homes in Zagreb? The atmosphere is different, and I want to come back and talk to you about it." My answer was, "We have Jesus." Again, I was so grateful the Lord had convicted me in time. What if I had been angry with these Muslim men trying to negotiate with one of my girls trying to get her baby.

One Sunday, one of our girls had come back from the Catholic church. She came to me in the kitchen, telling me she felt so empty and wanted what I had. I called Emina, who helped as our translator. For two hours, we shared Jesus. Danica accepted Jesus, and Emina said, "I did too as I translated for Esther." Both became strong believers, and God gave them both fine Christian husbands.

When Johnny and I returned every few years to Croatia to follow up on our women, Emina and Robert would drive us and interpret for us. The Lord worked it out that Robert would just happen to be home from his month at sea as an engineer when we needed their help. They often shared their testimony as they had lost three small children in tragic deaths, and their joy was so real despite their difficult circumstances. They led their families to the Lord, and we had the privilege of meeting them all. They even started a church in their hometown that, in the absence of a pastor, they are holding together. What a joy this couple has been to us through the years, especially when Donna joined me on my last trip after Johnny passed.

A couple of months after he passed, I was approached by John Clayton, SP Projects Director for Canada, to follow up with our women in Croatia since he had been our boss those years we were there. We started the trip with a weekend where several of the girls and their families joined us. Emina and Danica, the first two to accept the Lord in the home, shared with the others who had not yet met Jesus. Their husbands, who are strong Christians, also shared, and their lives were moved.

Donna had some precious one-on-one time with the twenty-four-year-olds who were born at our home. She also had an in-depth conversation with one of their dads on facetime, who couldn't make it to Zagreb with his wife and daughter. He told her he still had the shirt Johnny gave him when he escaped from the concentration camp and reunited with his wife at our home. Our women prayed for him every day at lunch that he would be released. He was able to escape and made it to the river, where a guard told him if he could swim across in five minutes to Croatia, he wouldn't shoot him. He found out thru friends, his wife was with us (our doctor met her in the hospital and brought her to us). When he got to us, he needed a shirt, trousers, and shoes that

Johnny supplied. What a testimony of answered prayer he was to our women.

After a busy weekend, we moved up across the border into Slovenia for a retreat of our own in Bled. Donna picked up a bug on the flight over to Frankfurt, where we had a mini-retreat with Izeta and her husband, who met us at the hotel. In Bled, Donna went to get a bite to eat in the restaurant and encountered a group she described as sheer evil, with blood-red pupils staring at her across the room. She woke up the next morning deathly ill. Emina and I did a lot of praying the next three days after a trip to the ER, where the doctor ordered bed rest. Donna reassured us her healing process would be completed when we got to Bosnia for the nurse from our home, Seka, to use one of her remedies on her.

Seka, being Muslim, had resisted the claims of Christ in her life, but now we could sense her peace. I gave her a miniature ceramic set of a Shepherd and four sheep that Natalie Willis in Boone had made as gifts for all the women. Seka pointed to the sheep and said she was one of them. That opened the door for us to share. Not long after our visit, Seka passed, and we feel confident she went to the arms of Jesus.

For the next ten days in Bosnia, we traveled to meet our women and their families. Manja, one of our girls, decided to follow Jesus when Donna confronted her by asking if she wanted to be set free of worry and have the peace that God gives. Her countenance turned from darkness to light almost instantaneously when she accepted Jesus! What a thrill to see! We felt the importance of seeing her on that trip. We just learned Manja passed on to be with Jesus after having a heart attack. That whole trip was so worth it because two more came to know Jesus before they passed to be in His glorious presence.

CHAPTER 31: OPERATION CHRISTMAS CHILD

"Clap your hands all you nations; shout to God with cries of joy" (Psalm 47:1, NIV).

A favorite project of ours every year was to shop and collect items for the shoeboxes we filled for Operation Christmas Child (OCC), a worldwide project of Samaritan's Purse. Nine million one hundred twenty-three thousand two hundred two boxes were distributed in 2020 to 120 countries, with approximately three and a half million children participating in The Greatest Journey Correspondence Course in discipleship programs in ninety-nine countries. Since we had been involved in distributions in Vietnam and Cambodia, we knew what gifts the children would like and always enjoyed doing our small part.

While we were in Croatia, shoe boxes were distributed in refugee camps in neighboring Bosnia. Relative children of our women were also recipients, and it brought them such joy. On our last trip back, one of the young men reminisced about how much it meant to him as a four-year-old to receive all those gifts in the shoe box.

One year we had the moving experience of going to Panama with the teams distributing throughout the village, in the countryside. The next time was in Vietnam. We were visiting our son David and family, missionaries with CAMA (and later World Vision) in Bangkok. SP asked us to join the teams in neighboring Cambodia and Vietnam.

I'll never forget the time a little girl, who had seen something so horrible, had stopped talking, but when she opened her box, and it had red shoes in them, she put them on and started talking and smiling and laughing with sheer delight.

Once, we were in a large government-run orphanage. The director asked us to join her in one of the buildings. Johnny was sitting on the floor playing cars with some of the boys. All of a sudden, I heard her excitedly calling me to come and see what the twins had received. One of the twins opened his box and showed me two pairs of pants, two pairs of underwear, and two t-shirts. The second twin showed me two sets of cars, pencils, crayons, etc. Wow! Two sets of everything! "Isn't this amazing," she exclaimed!

I had to be careful as we were in a Communist country. I looked at the group of onlookers that had gathered to see this foreign woman speaking in their language. I didn't know who was friend or foe. I figured it was my one chance to share and said, "Yes, it is amazing; I have a great God, and He knew who should get these taped, sealed boxes: these twins. Some lady in America prayed as she packed these boxes that just the right children would receive them, and our God answered her prayer."

A year later, we were back at the orphanage, and the lady came running out to the car to hug us. With tears in her eyes, she recounted the story of the twins. She took us to the reception room to distribute some sweaters we had brought and had four sets of twins join us. There were our two little boys! They were pleased to have their picture taken in their new sweaters.

Some days later, we arrived back home late in the evening and walked over to the home in our retirement village where the lady lived who had knit the sweaters. It was Christmas Eve, and her family had all gathered with her. She was thrilled to see her handiwork on eight little boys when we showed her the pictures, and she proudly showed her family. She was such a lovely, elegant lady. We always enjoyed our visits with her and would share with her as she was an amazing SP supporter and a dear friend. She had those moments of joy that last night we stopped in, and she passed on to her heavenly home the very next day. I am so glad we paid attention to God's nudging us to go visit her late that night upon arrival back home. God graciously had all of her family there for her last days, and they got to see the pictures of their mom's handiwork in those knitted sweaters.

There is a story I would like to share from Jonathan Hoa Tran: "I'm Jonathan, thirty-two years old, formerly a staff member of Samaritan's Purse, Vietnam. Twenty years ago, I was surviving as one of the many street children in the city and living in a shelter cared for by Samaritan's Purse, a Christian humanitarian organization. All of us were from different parts of Northern Vietnam, coming to Hanoi to earn our living by selling newspapers or working as shoeshine boys. Vietnamese society labeled us 'vulnerable subjects.' I didn't understand this term and didn't really care. I only wanted to know I could earn some money, enough to buy a meager meal instead of being hungry and having nothing to eat at home. My family was living in the northern mountainous region of Vietnam, bordering China, a remote mountainous wilderness.

"At age eleven, I dropped out of school after finishing Grade 5 due to extreme poverty and having to walk nine kilometers to school every day, a very long distance. My brother and I decided to quit school to stay home and help my parents doing farm work. We tried so hard for a few years but without any improvement in our financial situation. Then my brother was called to the army for military service, and my younger brother also dropped out of school. It seemed that I would never have a dream for the future.

"Out of despair, through the suggestion of a family friend, my parents allowed me to go with her to Hanoi with the hope that I could find a better future there.

"In 1996, after two months of living in the Samaritan's Purse shelter for street children, I received my first Operation Christmas Child shoebox. The first thing I pulled out of the box was a flute. (I know how to play the flute and really loved to play it when I was in my countryside.) I saw the very long candy with the smell of soap, which I had never tasted before…and the last thing I pulled out was a book of colored comics about a Christmas story with the pictures of sheep and camels…it was very strange to me. Understanding the meaning of the gift, I found out there is an existing 'unconditional love.' It came with love and compassion from Samaritan's Purse staff. The gift shoebox was small, but its power changed my life forever. Samaritan's Purse has been accessing many communities, many people, including myself. I came to know God through a Samaritan's Purse staff member and accepted Him in 1997.

"Thanks to the kindness of a scholarship from Samaritan's Purse Vietnam, I attended a special school for poor kids in Hanoi to finish high school. Eight of my classmates were blessed to receive His salvation through my testimony, as well as my family. Even though I have faced many difficulties, my parents have finally thrown away the family altar and have become very faithful Christians. Thank God for His mercy to His people. Between 1996 and 2001, the

Vietnamese government allowed double the amount of shoeboxes, 500,000 to one million, to be distributed to Vietnamese children. SP has become an important non-governmental organization helping thousands in poverty, with HIV/AIDS, with vulnerable people, as well as typhoons.

"I was able to study for two years of seminary in the Philippines, and my oldest brother, who was trained as a baker in a Samaritan's Purse vocational program, owns and operates his own small bakery and provides bread for hotels and restaurants in Sapa, a famous tourist site in the mountains. My parents and two youngest brothers now have a family farm with cattle, chicken, and fish. And I have my own family. Huyen, my lovely wife (my high school classmate), and a five-year-old son named Noah (he was born on the same day as the biggest flood more than eighty years ago).

"Thanks to our Jesus, we are saved. And it all started with a gift of love, the Operation Christmas Child shoebox given to a wide-eyed mountain child."

CHAPTER 32: DR. TUAN FINDS NELLY'S SILK PAINTING

"Finally, all of you be of one mind. Having compassion for one another; love as brothers, be tenderhearted, be courteous" (1 Peter 3:8, NKJV).

I received a letter from a Vietnamese doctor in California saying he had purchased, on eBay, a painting on silk of a bust of a Vietnamese woman. He took the frame off and found "1936" on the back and "1986 donated to Ridgeway Alliance Church, White Plains, NY, by Jake and Nelly Van Hine." The doctor wanted to know the background on this. One thousand nine hundred and thirty-six was when my parents bought it to use as a prop when speaking in churches in the US. One thousand nine hundred and eighty-six was when they gave it to the church to use in their missions conference.

He left his phone number in the letter, so I called him. He had so many questions, and we talked for hours in the days that followed. Dr. Tuan calls on a consistent basis to see how I am doing. He is like family. He and Donna have chatted many times. He thinks of her as his aunt. It's amazing how God brings people together.

Chapter 33: Meeting King Bao Dai

"The steps of a man are established by the LORD, when he delights in his way" (Psalm 37:23, ESV).

I know because my mother had the advantage of growing up in an affluent home and having social grace, she attracted many influential people and won several to the Lord. One highlight in my memories was being invited to dinner functions when someone dropped out, leaving thirteen at the table, a potential social faux pas! Since I was only between the ages of eight and ten, I took great pride in knowing which fork and knife to use during each course. I think this must be where I got my love of entertaining. I didn't inherit the artistic skills my mom learned at finishing school, but she taught me so much about entertaining.

One day especially stands out in my mind. I came in from school and was surprised to hear that "our" King Bao Dai was in town as I hadn't seen the flag flying over his summer palace, which indicated when the Emperor was home. His palace was adjacent to our Dalat School property. When the king's mother, who was having tea with my mother, overheard this little American girl refer to her son as "her" king, she was delighted. The next thing I knew was being arranged for his servant to open the back gate the next day to take me to meet "my king." Of course, my mom taught me to curtsey and speak in the third person. All my schoolmates were in shock the next day when his limousine brought me back to school in time for supper.

Chapter 34: Dad's Dream for the Yao Tribe Realized

"[…] I am the Lord. Now the blood shall be a sign for you on the houses where you are. And when I see the blood, I will pass over you; and the plague shall not be on you to destroy you when I strike the land of Egypt" (Exodus 12:12b–13, NKJV).

When I was a little girl in Indochina, I remember my dad being gone for some days, sometimes weeks, and returning home with bleeding feet; seeing this, I naturally had questions as I was inquisitive. He told me he walked for days up a mountain on the China border, trying to reach the Yao tribe that needed Jesus, but with no success. When they saw the white man coming, they ran from their village and hid in the jungle. Why the bleeding feet? In those days, there were no hiking boots, so he wore the flimsy tennis shoes of that day which gave no protection. My mother would nurse them, and off he'd go again.

Fast forward to when I was ten years old, my mom and I were sitting on the front row of the church, and this intoxicated man came staggering down the aisle and sat across the aisle from us in the men's section. This intrigued me. I remember it as if it was yesterday. My dad was preaching in Vietnamese, and my mom whispered, "That's not the sermon I heard him practicing all week.

It sounds like it's a broken record as he keeps repeating, 'The blood of Jesus, the blood of Jesus.'" At the close of the sermon, the man went to my dad, totally sober, and said he'd been in the market, heard some music, and followed it to the church. We knew he was a tribesman from his blue pajama-type clothing. He wanted to know more about the blood of Jesus as the sorcerer in the village told the people that someday they wouldn't have to shed the blood of animals, nor would they have to take blood from their wrist and offer it for protection from the evil spirits. Especially when they were sick, depending on the severity of their illness, the blood sacrifice could be anywhere from a chicken to a cow, which kept them poor. He was told someday, someone would shed his own blood for them.

So, this was good news to him. He wanted to take this news back to the mountain to the village chief and sorcerer. He did, and the following week, he brought them back to my dad and the Vietnamese pastor. They shared Jesus and how He shed His own blood on the cross for the forgiveness of their sins. What great news this was to the whole village when they were given this amazing news that they no longer had to take the blood and sprinkle it on the posts of their doors to appease the spirits to pass over and not harm them. Does that not remind you of the Bible story of the children of Israel killing a lamb, a representative of Jesus, and sprinkling its blood on their doorposts as protection for their firstborn child?

The whole village accepted Jesus as Savior, and a few weeks later, they all walked the long trek to our town and attended the special Christmas celebration. That Christmas in 1938 was my favorite Christmas. The French officials thought it was an uprising of this village against the government as they had tried for years to reach them to do a census, but they'd escape to the jungle! Sound familiar?

Today, there are 30,000 Yao tribespeople that have turned from their idols to enjoy the peace in their hearts of having Jesus live in their lives. They just recently celebrated eighty years of being believers. The tribal leaders had invited David to bring me to North Vietnam to celebrate with them because my dad had trekked up into the mountains to share Jesus with them, but with the COVID-19, that wasn't possible, much to our dismay. I remember as a child seeing my mother after each trip bandaging my dad's bleeding feet. (He didn't have proper shoes back in 1938, but that didn't stop him.)

A unique and wonderful bond was formed in New Jersey that would affect the Yao tribes years later. This happened when my mom was speaking in a Bronx mission in New York and telling their story. A dear couple, the John Mygatts, heard her speak and invited my parents to their home for Sunday dinner, and as a result, it became a tradition for many years.

Ethel Kleist was included in their group, a dear friend of the Mygatts. As a result, she gave me my first real summer job when I was sixteen at a prominent Wall Street insurance company where she was an executive.

The Mygatts and Ethel loved hearing my parents' stories about their Vietnam ministry, especially the stories about the Yao tribe. Ethel Kleist had made Bunny Mygatt executor of her will. A large amount of money was designated for the Yao ministry. Bunny contacted me, and I told her SP could handle the finances of this transaction, and in turn, we put them in touch with our son David who was having regular contact with the Yao leadership in Vietnam and could tell Bunny and SP where this amount of money could be most effectively used.

It was agreed there was a need for simple chapel structures to be built throughout the mountains of North Vietnam where the Yao could meet and invite their neighbors. There were also many simple structures in need of new roofs and sides.

Money was also given to the seminary, along with money in lieu of flowers when Johnny passed, to help Dao students in Hanoi who could not graduate and receive their diplomas because they had debt.

Tribal

CHAPTER 35: GIRL SOLD BY HER MOM AT FIFTEEN INTO PROSTITUTION

St. Francis of Assisi said, "Preach the gospel all the time if necessary, use words."

Several years ago, while at our son's home in Bangkok, Thailand, we received a call from our SP Canadian director, John Clayton, who had just left us a few days earlier on his way to Cambodia. He said we needed to fly over, just an hour, to Phnom Penh from Bangkok and encourage our C&MA missionary couple, Rick and Beth Drummond, to work with the Vietnamese in Phnom Penh.

Again, I was so thankful for the privilege of having served God those many years in Vietnam, knew the language, and could assist them in their heavy schedule. Here there were 100,000 displaced Vietnamese people in Cambodia, many of them in the Phnom Penh city area, living over garbage dumps in houses, really platforms, built on stilts. Their conditions were appalling. We felt almost physically ill as we walked through garbage and human excretion to get to the different homes Rick and Beth wanted us to visit.

We came to a young twenty-one-year-old's home, just a platform. I climbed up the rickety ladder and sat on the floor with her on her mat, put my arm around her as we talked, and shared and prayed. She was just skin and bones, a beautiful girl when she smiled but had little to smile about as her mother had sold her at age fifteen to a prostitution house for $300 so the rest of the family would be able to eat. They left her, promising to come back someday and buy her back, but here five years later, she is dying of AIDS.

I thought, *How could a mother do this to her daughter?* The daughter seemed to have such peace, and that was because Beth had shared Jesus with her and was teaching her the gospel truths, along with several other girls like her. She was there on Sunday when we preached in Vietnamese. My heart just broke for her.

At a Vietnamese ladies meeting at Beth's home, a woman that we had met earlier teaching children in one of the four rooms used as a classroom in the different neighborhoods during the day, and church on Sunday, shared with me her conversion story. She pointed to a woman in the group who had shown love to her by caring for her newborn baby. The baby cried day and night and thus could not eat, and if she did, she threw it all back up. The mother was desperate and had to get out selling her dried bananas as her husband didn't have a job, and it was almost impossible to find work there. She had tried to find a woman who would take her child, but no one wanted that responsibility thinking the child was going to die anyway, and then the spirits would attack them. One day she went by a house where the baby was crying incessantly, actually abandoned by the babysitter, and she took the child home and started caring for it. When the mother returned from the upcountry, she found the stranger caring for her child, and the child was no longer crying. She said she prayed three days and three nights to her God that this baby would stop crying, and the lady's prayers were answered. Through the love this Christian woman had shown her, she and her husband accepted Christ.

Rick and Beth's dedication to helping these Vietnamese people in Cambodia is remarkable. They were assigned to Cambodia for their Vietnamese language skills and served many years there. Today, as a result of their ministry, there are four churches in the slums in Phnom Penh.

CHAPTER 36: FIX OUR EYES ON JESUS

"Keep away from anything that might take God's place in your hearts" (John 5:21, NLT).

I think of all the Vietnamese I have known through the years who have given up their worship of Buddha to follow Jesus. One day in Bangkok, I was standing at the entrance of the temple where people were kneeling prostrate on the floor in worship of a thousand-pound golden Buddha. I was saddened, as the Buddha had eyes but couldn't see, ears but couldn't hear, a mouth that couldn't speak, and nose that couldn't smell, and hands and feet that couldn't be used. Then, in contrast, I thought of the thousands that have turned from their idols and have trusted in Jesus, their Savior, their helper, their shield:

> Therefore, since we are surrounded by such a great cloud of witnesses, let us throw off everything that hinders and the sin that so easily entangles. And let us run with perseverance the race marked out for us, fixing our eyes on Jesus, the pioneer and perfecter of faith. For the joy set before him, he endured the cross, scorning its shame, and sat down at the right hand of the throne of God.
>
> Hebrews 12:1–2 (NIV)

This promise of God's presence is powerful. There are pitfalls in our journey through life, but He promises to be with us always.

Chapter 37: Reflections

I woke up at 1:00 this morning, and my thoughts went to the final chapter. I am so aware of God's goodness through the years and the many opportunities for service. I am so grateful for the four children God gave us.

Johnny's strong solid character is reflected in many ways in his sons. Mel is so understanding and kind when working with those who have addictions. Due to the anonymity of the groups, I don't think I'm supposed to mention them. His mission field is here in the States. He reminds me so much of Johnny when he was a pastor. Mel couldn't have done it alone. He has been married to Linda, a nurse, for thirty-one years, and they have a beautiful daughter, Marlee, who has her bachelor's in psychology. It has been so special living near them these many years in Florida.

I mentioned before our son David is working in Thailand with his wife, Karen, who is gifted at teaching kids English online. Karen is involved with various women's ministries with the Evangelical Church of Bangkok. David does special projects with Vietnam. He, like Johnny, has faithfully served the Lord for forty-two years. His ministry is Kingdom. He has interviewed many missionaries documenting their work.

Johnny exhibited such discipline, and I see this in Mark. He recently retired from a federal job after thirty-five years. He quietly worked behind the scenes on million-dollar projects while others stood in the limelight. One time, Donna asked him why he wasn't at a press conference where he oversaw a big project. He said he would rather be behind the scenes. This reminded me so much of something Johnny would say. Donna told me the head of intelligence who ran the refugee camps told her at a function they had observed Johnny for some time and had a rather large "file" on him to see if he was "in it for recognition" before allowing him into the dockyard, where security was tight as it was the first camp where they lived and were tightly screened. Mark has been so fortunate to have Chris in his life. They have been married thirty-nine years and have two great kids, Liam and Maia. Maia is working for the Department of Health in New York City, and Liam is in Germany working on his doctorate in microbiology.

Donna, our daughter, and I now live together in Port Orange, Florida. Donna didn't want to see me eventually end up in a nursing home. When Johnny was alive, she loved doting on him as she worked just down the road from us in Kissimmee. She has expressed so often her gratitude for the modeling Johnny demonstrated to her son, Jean Claude, who is now a psychiatrist in Alaska. Johnny and Jean Claude formed a close bond over the chessboard. We will never know for sure if Grandpa really "let Jean Claude win."

We have been so fortunate to have Johnny's sister, Ruth, and her husband, Don (Olson), living in a retirement village close by. This has afforded us, especially in recent years with our move to Deland a few months before Johnny's passing, the opportunity to get together more often. Ruth and Don are so supportive and helpful.

So many have shared over the years what an amazing counselor Johnny was to them. When an administrator, the staff valued the way he was a buffer for them with his gentle manner.

We shared so many humorous and even embarrassing moments and enjoyed reminiscing over the years. One funny story was when Johnny and Franklin Irwin (also a Dalat MK) were upcountry in Central Vietnam for a couple of weeks of preaching in an area that had not heard the gospel. They stayed at a local home of a man who owned a popsicle business. One day he gave Johnny and Franklin a tour of the process he had in making popsicles. First, he showed them the water tank, and there, to their horror, was floating a big water-soaked rat. The two men had just eaten twelve of the finger-sized sticks as they came in from a hot morning of preaching and being very thirsty. No one was sick. To this day, when I see popsicles, I remember how this must have felt. I remind Franklin, as he's ninety-eight and retired in Toronto, and we have a good laugh!

One embarrassing story was about our pastors who loved getting together for a dog feast. When our pastor asked for our dog when we were leaving for the US for furlough, it was with the stipulation there would not be a dog feast. We left for Saigon to board our ship, but due to a delay, we returned to our mission station. Much to the surprise of our pastor, our dog was nowhere to be found.

Chapter 38: I'm Thankful for This Year of COVID-19 with Time to Be Still and Know that He Is God

I'm grateful for the unexpected gift of my ninety-second year, so I can see how God has blessed my four children and seven precious grandchildren. They, in turn, have given me four darling little great-granddaughters and great-grandson!

I woke up very early on August 21, 2020, thinking about two early birthday cards I received for my ninety-first birthday. Sam McGuinn, our former boss at Samaritan's Purse, quoted Isaiah 46:4 (NIV), "Even to your old age and gray hairs I am he, I am he who will sustain you. I have made you, and I will carry you; I will sustain you, and I will rescue you."

I am instantly reminded of how apropos the last part of this verse is when it comes to a couple of years ago when I was crippled with back pain and was on the trip to Boone to walk alongside the Vietnamese chefs working there. The Adams were my hosts. (Doctor Adams moved quickly and made decisions as Jean Claude's pediatrician thirty years ago and, as a result, saved Jean Claude's life, Donna's son, when he was born). Now I was in need of his help. He put me in the hands of amazing doctors and took care of me. They have been such great friends all these years. It was Donna

Toney's doctor, Franklin's assistant, that, after a surgical procedure on my lower back, put me back into commission. During my time in Boone, my immediate boss, Angela Smith, and our boss Steve Nichol made sure, along with Louise Stout, my assistant, that I was beautifully cared for. I was overwhelmed with their kindness, making sure all my needs were met. That just doesn't happen in the norm. They waited on me hand and foot. I am so grateful for each one of them.

Now, getting back to the content of the second card from missionary friends living in the Deland Alliance community, Dr. Fred and Helen Polding said, "Flourish like a tree in 2020." The verse quoted Psalm 52:8 (NKJV), "But I am like a green olive tree in the house of God; I trust in the mercy of God forever and ever." I was aware again of the many friends who had been insisting that we write a book, but my husband's response was that there are already so many books out there. But this morning, I was reminded that God has spared my years through difficult but beautiful times. I am so blessed, also, during this time to have such amazing neighbors who I can rely on, Arleen McCartney and Joan Matteson. Joan is a nurse, and one time when I had a deep wound I had gotten from a heating pad, she came in daily and dressed the wound. I am so fortunate to have Joan and Arleen.

During this pandemic, how well was I using these days of being set aside? I have certainly had time to reflect and "be still and know that He is God." When I spoke to my missionary friend, he prayed, thanking God for my years of *doing* His will and now for *being* in His will. *How do I then flourish as the card indicated?* I was reminded of three words that meant so much to my husband and me in our sixty-seven years of marriage and ministry: *available, flexible, and adaptable.* They continue to have an impact on me, especially as I am still working for Samaritans Purse and need to be *available* to people's needs as I call them and thank them for their donations on behalf of Franklin Graham, for example, I got a prayer request that said "depression." I called and got an answering machine and felt led to do something I had never done (being *flexible*), and that was to pray on the answering machine (being *adaptable*) that Jesus, the light of the world, would penetrate the dark cloud hovering over her and permeate her mind and whole being.

A year later, I called her to thank her for a recent donation. When she became aware I was the one who had prayed on her answering machine, she shared that she was driving back to Florida from Georgia when she felt that burden totally lift, one that she had carried eight years since her husband's death. When she got home and listened to my prayer on her answering machine, she knew it was the exact time the burden lifted. This is a constant reminder these past years of God's power as I continue in Samaritan's Purse phone ministry, grateful I'm still alive and strong to serve. If God uses me for just one person, it makes it all worthwhile. I recently read that one in three seniors die within one year of breaking their hip. It's hard sometimes to believe I had such a bad break back in 2009. He has carried me to the other side of so many barriers.

Psalm 92:12–15 (TLB) is such an encouragement and promise:

> But the godly shall flourish like palm trees and grow tall as the cedars of Lebanon, for they are transplanted into the Lord's own garden and are under his personal care. Even in old age, they still produce fruit and are vital and green. This honors the Lord and exhibits his faithful care. He is my shelter. There is nothing but goodness in him!

It is my heart's desire in my old age to produce fruit and be vital.

Nightly, as I am going to sleep, I continue Johnny's and my tradition of quoting Psalm 23:

> The LORD is my shepherd; I shall not want. He maketh me to lie down in green pastures: he leadeth me beside the still waters, He restoreth my soul: he leadeth me in the paths of righteousness for his name's sake. Yea, though I walk through the valley of the shadow of death, I will fear no evil; for though art with me; thy rod and thy staff they comfort me. Thou preparest a table in the presence of mine enemies: thou anointest my head with oil; my cup runneth over. Surely goodness and mercy shall follow me all the days of my life: and I will dwell in the house of the LORD for ever.
>
> Psalm 23:1–6 (KJV)

I ponder on each phrase getting new insights, blessed by the promises, and challenged to live pleasing to the Lord. I leave you with this twenty-third psalm, hoping you let Him permeate your heart and mind. Thank you for letting me share my stories of how God has walked beside me, carried me, and sustained me all the days of my life, whether I was cognizant of it or not, so beautifully crisscrossing our lives across continents. Love to all of you who have meant so much to Johnny and me throughout the years. Thank you for working alongside us for His kingdom. Even though I didn't get to acknowledge everyone, just know you are in my heart, and I love you and appreciate you.

Esther.